"Reading these insightful and incisive interventions is nothing short of watching a master at work in the studio. Everything that crosses Brueggemann's desk, is read by his eyes, or occurs to his incomparable brain is sieved through Scripture—all for our betterment with equal measures of judgment and hope. Taste and see, watch and learn. Then go and do likewise."
—BRENT A. STRAWN, D. Moody Smith Distinguished Professor of Old Testament and Professor of Law, Duke University

"In this fascinating and generative new collection of essays, Walter Brueggemann seamlessly moves from the world of the text into the world we inhabit today, fearlessly telling the difficult truths and proclaiming the gospel with wild abandon, refusing to get caught in meaningless minutiae or waste anyone's time with 'small gains in yardage.' From new economic theories to fresh takes on contemporary political issues and innovative interpretations of biblical texts, Brueggemann yet again freely shares the fruits of his voracious mind, compassionate heart, and faithful spirit."
—BRENNAN BREED, associate professor of Old Testament, Columbia Theological Seminary

"Brueggemann critiques today's political gaslighting, perpetual debt servitude, petty self-absorptions, and self-serving systems, but then pivots to that lamp unto our feet, of prophetic lyrics illumining our way forward, calling us to join divine urgency for justice, righteousness, and compassion for all our neighbors. Following a more indigenous path, listening to nature's praise, Walter laments for the languishing earth, but assures her dawn will come."
—NANCY C. LEE, professor of Hebrew Bible, Elmhurst University

"Required reading for these critical times. In these remarkable reflections, Walter Brueggemann invites us to relinquish faith in our vain 'little systems,' to rediscover the deep relationship between grief and imagination, and to embrace a biblical theology that is alive and responsive and refuses to settle."
—TIMOTHY BEAL, distinguished university professor, Case Western Reserve University

Lament *That Generates* Covenant

Lament *That Generates* Covenant

And Other Essays

WALTER BRUEGGEMANN

CASCADE *Books* • Eugene, Oregon

LAMENT THAT GENERATES COVENANT
And Other Essays

Copyright © 2025 Walter Brueggemann. All rights reserved. Except for brief quotations in critical publications or reviews, no part of this book may be reproduced in any manner without prior written permission from the publisher. Write: Permissions, Wipf and Stock Publishers, 199 W. 8th Ave., Suite 3, Eugene, OR 97401.

Cascade Books
An Imprint of Wipf and Stock Publishers
199 W. 8th Ave., Suite 3
Eugene, OR 97401

www.wipfandstock.com

PAPERBACK ISBN: 979-8-3852-1771-7
HARDCOVER ISBN: 979-8-3852-1772-4
EBOOK ISBN: 979-8-3852-1773-1

Cataloguing-in-Publication data:

Names: Brueggemann, Walter, author.

Title: Lament that generates covenant : and other essays / Walter Brueggemann.

Description: Eugene, OR: Cascade Books, 2025. | Includes bibliographical references and indexes.

Identifiers: ISBN 979-8-3852-1771-7 (paperback). | ISBN 979-8-3852-1772-4 (hardcover). | ISBN 979-8-3852-1773-1 (ebook).

Subjects: LCSH: Bible—Criticism, interpretation, etc. | Bible—Homiletical use. | Political theology.

Classification: BS1192.5 B825 2025 (print). | BS1192.5 (ebook).

02/25/25

Scripture quotations are from New Revised Standard Version of the Bible, copyright © 1989 by the National Council of the Churches of Christ in the United States of America. Used by permission. All rights reserved worldwide.

Contents

Preface | vii

1. A Small Gain in Yardage | 1
2. Beyond the Spreadsheet | 7
3. Bondage: Serve and Owe | 15
4. Borne Away | 23
5. Discriminatory Gaslighting | 29
6. Lament that Generates Covenant | 37
7. Majoring in Minors | 39
8. O Land, Land, Land | 45
9. Our Little Systems! | 48
10. Providential Tyranny | 54
11. Psalm 29 | 62
12. Psalm 107:1–3, 17–22 | 67
13. Refusing Erasure | 72
14. Return to Normal? | 78
15. Snow as Testimony | 85
16. Solidarity that Counts | 92
17. The "Ands" of the Gospel | 97
18. The Conditions from Which the Poems Arose | 104
19. The McCarthy Cousins | 113
20. The Peaceful Transfer of Real Power | 120

Contents

21 Traitor to Your Class | 125

22 We Will Get Through This Together | 133

23 When the Music Starts Again | 138

Bibliography | 145

Scripture Index | 149

Name Index | 151

Preface

THIS COLLECTION OF REFLECTIONS ranges over a number of my abiding interests. It is my hope that each reflection is both well-grounded in Scripture, and effectively linked to our present daily life that summons us to faith. It is clear in my title essay that "covenant" signifies the core claim of Scripture, that is, solidarity between the creating, saving God and the world that God loves and calls into being, and solidarity between human persons and human communities. This accent is reflected as well in my essay, "Solidarity that Lasts," and in my theme, "through this together." Covenantal solidarity is constituted both by the gifts of the covenant-creating God and by the sustained effort through generative human initiative.

This accent on covenantal solidarity is, of course, a contradiction of the common assumptions and practices of Western political economy that much too easily takes the individual as the defining unit of human life. Such an assumption of individualism is, inescapably, an invitation to anxiety, greed, and violence, because every other human agent is readily perceived as a rival or even as a threat. Against such an assumption, covenantal solidarity begins with the assumption that "the other" is a neighbor who is bound with us in solidarity. It is the insistence of faith against the idolatry of individualism that meaning and social possibility are grounded in community, and in the generous sharing of resources that make life livable and sustainable. At the most elemental levels of human existence, it is easy enough to see such solidarity as communities regularly rally, across every ideological boundary, in times of emergency. The problem is to evoke and sustain such practice of solidarity for continuing emergencies that lack dramatic power but that admit of no easy solution or disposal.

My essay "When the Music Starts Again" is a meditation on the abyss of the exile and deportation of ancient Israel when the lights went out in Jerusalem, and all the music stopped as life yielded to massive imperial power. It

Preface

belongs to the prophet Jeremiah to mark the dramatic moment of restoration when public life could be resumed in Jerusalem and in its temple. The music could have been great doxologies to God, but here it is the joyous sound of wedding celebration that marks the possibility of an ordered societal life.

Thus in all of these essays, the background assumption is that social life can be and has been massively disrupted. In prophetic tradition, moreover, it is characteristically affirmed that the God who sanctions such disruption is also the God who manages and empowers restoration and the rehabilitation of social life. Thus the music that accompanies the historical process is the practice of celebrative doxologies, the sad lamentations of loss and displacement, and the restoration of celebrative singing and dancing. Both musical cadences, celebrative and lamenting, live close to the life that Israel experienced and both attest to the reality of God as the one who governs and oversees Israel's life in the world.

It is easy enough to see that the sum of celebration and lamentation pertain to our common contemporary life as well. In actual practice, moreover, the community of faith does much better at celebration than it does with lamentation that admits loss and that credits loss to the rule of God. Thus one of the continuing challenges for the faith community, in its liturgy and in its piety, is to develop forms and practices of lamentation that are closely in touch with our lived experience. It is my hope that these several essays will provide resources and motivation for the necessary work of development of a piety of vulnerability, for it is exactly the practice of such vulnerability that makes covenant both possible and urgent.

It remains for me to thank the three people who make my ongoing work possible. First and foremost, Tia Brueggemann is a steady hand of critical support for my work, most especially with her keen editorial eye. Mary Brown guides the blog site where many of these pieces have first appeared. And K. C. Hanson, yet again, has been a selfless support to see my work through to publication. I am profoundly grateful to all three of these defining presences in my work life.

It is my primary insistence that when our common life is framed in the categories of biblical faith with its confidence in the rule of God, everything is recharacterized. It is this defining reference in faith that very differently identifies God's gifts to us and that very differently calls out the duties to which we are summoned.

Walter Brueggemann
December 18, 2024

1

A Small Gain in Yardage

IN HIS NEW BIOGRAPHY of John Steinbeck, William Souder, *Mad at the World: A Life of John Steinbeck*, portrays his subject as a hard-living writer who placed heavy demands upon himself and upon those around him. In addition to his relentless passion for good writing, he had a sporadic passion for great drinking and for great womanizing. Among his passions is his deep abhorrence for any bully as is evidenced in his *The Grapes of Wrath* and the predatory bullying done by the California growers. Given his careless self-destructiveness, his friends often urged Steinbeck to modify his strong living:

> Slow down, lose weight, watch your cholesterol, and remember, you're not as young you used to be.[1]

Steinbeck would have none of it. He responded to such advice:

> For I have always lived violently, drunk hugely, eaten too much or not at all, slept around the clock or missed two nights of sleeping, worked too hard and too long in glory, or slobbed for a time in utter laziness. I've lifted, pulled, chopped, climbed, made love with joy and taken my hangovers as a consequence, not as a punishment. I did not want to surrender fierceness for a small gain of yardage.[2]

I am much taken with his contrast and juxtaposition of his "fierceness" and his notion of "a small gain in yardage." I take the latter phrase to mean that

---

1. Souder, *Mad at the World*, 351.
2. Souder, *Mad at the World*, 351.

he might live a bit longer if he took better care of himself. But he refused to consider such small gains in "yardage" if it would require curbing his fierce living.

Without suggesting that anyone should emulate Steinbeck's particular modes of "fierceness," his defiant statement got me to thinking about a sense of priority as is commended in the gospel narrative. Steinbeck's statement reminded me of two statements credited to Jesus, even if they are very different from Steinbeck's particularities. What follows here is a brief reflection on these two statements and their sense of life priorities.

In his Sermon on the Mount Jesus invites his listeners away from "gaining yardage" about food or drink or clothing or housing, or "adding a single hour to your span of life" (Matt 6:25-27; Luke 12:22-25). These are not, in his purview, proper worries. Better, he urges, to devote one's energy to the "kingdom of God and his righteousness" (Matt 6:33). The verb for this summons is "strive," no doubt an alternative to "be anxious." The summons is to be actively engaged in God's future, and not to be distracted with personal worry. This dictum does not specify "Kingdom of God" but of course his entire enterprise of teaching is an exposition of the coming alternative governance of God that is marked by generosity, forgiveness, and hospitality. That future cannot be given a blueprint but can only be educed by story and specific act.

It seems to me legitimate to let Steinbeck's "fierceness" be rendered as "striving for the kingdom" and his "small gain of yardage" as a measure for anxiety about food, drink, clothing, housing, and length of days. If we accept this equivalence, *mutatis mutandis*, then Jesus calls his disciples to a singular passion for "the kingdom" and away from more mundane anxieties. He said this to his disciples, in the sequence of Matthew, just after he had declared to them:

> No one can serve two masters; for a slave will either hate the one
> and love the other, or be devoted to the one and despise the other.
> You cannot serve God and wealth. (Matt 6:24; see Luke 16:13)

This is an either/or as stark as the one Steinbeck had discerned. The "fierceness" to which Jesus calls his disciples is an elusive alternative society of neighborliness. In appealing to Steinbeck's "fierceness" we may get a fresh notion of Jesus' "passion." We readily speak of his "passion story" concerning his journey to the cross and we convert Palm Sunday into "Passion Sunday," by which we refer to his upcoming arrest, trial, and execution. If, however, we take "passion" in a more popular sense, we can see that Jesus had a peculiar passion for the coming alternative neighborhood and would not be distracted from it; he intends, moreover, that his disciples join in this passion with fierceness.

The other text that occurs to me from Steinbeck's either/or is Jesus' radical summons to discipleship in Matt 16:24–28; Mark 8:34—9:1; Luke 9:23–27):

> For those who want to save their life will lose it, and those who lose their life for my sake will find it. For what will it profit them if they gain the whole world but forfeit their life? Or what will they gain in return for their life? (Matt 6:25–26)

In this statement Jesus juxtaposes "world" and "life," a curious either /or. By "world" he refers to the available sphere of possessable objects . . . not unlike the food and clothing of Matthew 6. By "life" he apparently means the identifiable, fragile personal self in the image of God. Again the either/or is radical and uncompromising; we cannot have both. The possession of the "whole world" leads to the diminishment of life: or in the words of the hymn, we become "rich in things and poor is soul."

Both the either/or of Jesus in Matt 6:25–26 and Matt 16:24–28, and the either/or of Steinbeck of "fierceness" or "a gain of small yardage," summons us to clear critical thinking about the purpose of our lives. This deep either/or (an echo of Moses in Deut 30:20 and of Joshua in Josh 24:14–15) permeates the biblical tradition. This deep either/or seems to me particularly pertinent in our society that is preoccupied with matters of safety, wellbeing, and longevity. And of course these matters have become even more acute with the pandemic. But even without regard to the pandemic, our consumer culture has made our *selves* and our *bodies* into objects to be protected and cared for with demanding attentiveness. No doubt some of that attentiveness is normal and natural. If, however, we may judge from the endless ads on TV for cosmetic supplies and drugs, we might think that our society is obsessed with "small gains of yardage," that our lives and our bodies might be extended a bit further in their beauty and power. This obsessive concern (that justifies the aggressive marketing of stuff we did not know we needed for our wellbeing) drives out any readiness for risk for the common good, that is, for the kingdom of God's righteousness.

What is at stake in these uncompromising either/or statements in the gospel is the long-term purpose of human life. One cannot and would not want to object, I suppose, to responsible healthy self-care. But when it becomes a central preoccupation of our lives, as aggressive consumerism would have it become, then the work of the common good evaporates from our horizon.

I finish with a reflection on the first question of the catechism in which I was nurtured, *The Evangelical Catechism* of the *Evangelical Synod of North America*, an antecedent of the United Church of Christ. In the edition of the catechism that I memorized, the first question is: "What should be the chief concern of man?"[3] The gender specificity of course reflects the patriarchal assumptions of the time of the edition. The catechism has happily been freshly translated by Frederick R. Trost, *The Evangelical Catechism: A New Translation for the 21st Century*. The answer in the catechism that I learned is this:

> Man's chief concern should be to seek after the Kingdom of God and his righteousness.

The supportive texts for that answer given in the catechism are exactly the two I have cited:

> Seek ye first his kingdom, and his righteousness; and all these things shall be added unto you. (Matt 6:33)

> For what shall a man be profited, if he shall gain the whole world and forfeit his life? Or what shall a man give in exchange for his life? (Matt 16:26)

It interests me that in an earlier version of the catechism that begins with the same question offers a very different answer: "Man's chief concern should be the eternal salvation of his soul." The contrast of the two answers is stunning. It seems clear that this radical revision of the answer was under the impetus of the "social gospel," in my ecclesial tradition represented in those days by the brothers Niebuhr. It is evident that the two alternative answers represent very different theological perspectives. The more "pietistic" answer ("eternal salvation of the soul") sounds a little like "a gain of yardage," whereas to seek God's kingdom and righteousness is a summons to a fierceness beyond one's self. The contrast between the answers, of course, is not so sharp when the answers are situated in the context of German pietism that always understood that *one's salvation* was deeply linked to *God's righteousness*.

The question posed by the catechism belongs centrally to human consciousness. It is the overriding question of human existence. It is, at the

---

3. *Evangelical Catechism*, 11.

same time, a question peculiarly entrusted to the church (and its companion communities). We live in a consumer society that is every day offering an answer to the question, an answer that concerns "small gains of yardage." But lives that pivot on such small gains of yardage do not yield any fierceness for justice, righteousness, compassion, or mercy, do not factor out into practices of generosity, forgiveness, and hospitality. It is for good reason that the church, from the ground up, gives answer to the question in a way that refuses the answer of our culture. We sing hymns, pray prayers, study texts, and listen to good news proclamations in order to host the alternative answer of the gospel. These disciplines are not in order to gain yardage. They are, rather, in order to inhale the fierceness that belongs to our true humanity. Steinbeck would have been completely impatient with the church's attempt to sort this out. He understood, nevertheless, that the question posed by the catechism is an important one. He answered it with his fierce writing. A major moment of that fierce writing that was for him a moment of fierce living came for Steinbeck in *The Grapes of Wrath*. In that fierce book, he wrote nothing more humanely fierce than its conclusion, a conclusion that proved to be too fiercely bodily for the film version of the novel. In response to the sick, starving man they discovered in the rainstorm in the barn at the end of the story, Ma guides Rose of Sharon to fierce self-giving:

> For a minute Rose of Sharon sat still in the whispering barn. The she hoisted her tired body up and drew the comfort about her. She moved slowly to the corner and stood looking down at the wasted face, into the wide, frightened eyes. Then slowly she lay down beside him. He shook his head slowly from side to side. Rose of Sharon loosened one side of the blanket and bared her breast. "You got to," she said. She squirmed closer and pulled his head close. "There!" she said. "There." Her hand moved behind his head and supported it. Her fingers moved gently in his hair. She looked up and across the barn, and her lips came together and smiled mysteriously.[4]

The self-giving act of Rose of Sharon sounds like an echo of Matthew 25:

> I was hungry and you gave me food, I was thirsty and you gave me something to drink, I was a stranger and you welcomed me, I was naked and you gave me clothing. I was sick and you took care of me, I was in prison and you visited me . . . Truly I tell you, just

---

4. Steinbeck, *The Grapes of Wrath*, 580–81.

> as you did it to one of the least of these who are members of my family, you did it to me. (Matt 25:35–36, 40)

This sick, desperate man was surely "the least." Steinbeck, in his fierceness, has Rose of Sharon provide the hungry man with food from her body. The act of Rose of Sharon required her to turn away from any thought of "extra yardage" in order to perform her generous bodily fierceness, all for the sake of an unnamed neighbor.

2

Beyond the Spreadsheet

NEWS ITEM:

> After years of dire predictions that failed to pan out, the people who run fiscal and monetary policy in Washington have decided the risk of "overheating" the economy is much lower than a risk of failing to heat it up enough... Many economist have déjà vu when it comes to overheating warnings.[1]

The linkage between the God of the Gospel and economics is deep, wide, and inescapable. One cannot have the God of the Gospel without the neighborly economy willed by the God of the Gospel. For Roman Catholics, see the social teaching of Pope Leo XIII, *Rerum novarum*. For Lutherans, see *The Forgotten Luther: Reclaiming the Social-Economic Dimension of the Reformation* edited by Carter Lindberg and Paul Wee. For Calvinists, see André Biéler, *Calvin's Economic and Social Thought*. That linkage nowhere has been made more compellingly than by M. Douglas Meeks, *God the Economist: The Doctrine of God and Political Economy*, who shows that our term "economy" comes from the Greek *oikos* (household) and that God is the ultimate "householder" who provides all that is needed for the "household" of creation:

> As a way of correlating God and economy I propose the term *oikos*. In the broadest sense I will mean by *oikos* access to livelihood. The household living relationships of the *oikos* are the institutional relationships aimed at the survival of human beings in society. *Oikos*

---

1. Tankersley and Smialek, "Inflation Fears," A1.

is the way persons dwell in the world toward viability in relation to family, state, market, nature and God. *Oikos* is the heart of both ecclesiology and political economy.[2]

In order to consider this linkage between *God and economy* I appeal to the familiar benediction of Eph 3:20–21 wherein the writer celebrates, in doxological cadence, God's unparalleled capacity for abundant accomplishment:

> Now to him who by the power at work within us is able to accomplish abundantly far more than all we can ask or imagine, to him be glory in the church and in Christ Jesus to all generations, forever and ever. Amen.

This doxological benediction affirms that God's gracious and generous capacity is beyond every limit of human imagination. God has a limitless capacity to do good and provide good in and for and through all creation. This affirmation recurs in the doxological Psalms:

> These all look to you
>   to give them their food in due season;
> when you give it to them, they gather it up;
>   when you open your hand, they are filled with good things.
> (Ps 104:27–28)

> The eyes of all look to you,
>   and you give them their food in due season.
> You open your hand,
>   satisfying the desire of every living thing. (Ps 145:15–16)

> He determines the number of the stars;
>   he gives to all of them their names.
> Great is our Lord, and abundant in power;
>   his understanding is beyond measure.
> The Lord lifts up the downtrodden;
>   he casts the wicked to the ground.
> Sing to the Lord with thanksgiving;
>   make melody to our God on the lyre.
> He covers the heavens with clouds,
>   prepares the rain for the earth,
>   makes grass to grow on the hills.
> He gives to the animals their food,
>   and to the young ravens when they cry . . .

---

2. Meeks, *God the Economist*, 33.

> He gives snow like wool;
> > he scatters frost like ashes,
>
> He hurls down hail like crumbs—
> > who can stand before his cold"?
>
> He sends out his word and melts them;
> > he makes winds blow and the waters flow. (Ps 147:4–9, 16–18)

The "household" of creation is assured an ample provision that outruns every calculation. It belongs to the capacity of the creator God to outrun our best expectations and estimations. God's generative capacity provides that God's good creation is a gift that keeps on giving.

It is of course decisively interesting that in the doxological benediction of Eph 3:20–21 it is attested that his generous provision outruns all that we can ask. We make our petitions in our need and find that God answers beyond our need or our petition (see Matt 7:7–11). More than that, it is attested that this generous provision outruns all that we can "imagine." The Greek term *noeo* suggests not only "imagine," but "comprehend" or "understand." If we stay with the conventional translation, "imagine," this affirmation means that human imagination is too restricted, domesticated, and contained to embrace the expansive wonder of God's generative capacity.

I can think of two texts in which the narrative shows that the generativity of God requires Israel to reach beyond the limits of its imagination in order to receive God's abundance. (There are no doubt many other such texts and indeed the "miracles" of Jesus attest that God's power for life runs well beyond human imagination.) In the manna narrative of Exodus 16, there is a desperate need for bread and water in the wilderness, for the wilderness is precisely a place without resources (Exod 16:3). Israel could not imagine such provision in the wilderness. In response to their complaint, "bread from heaven" is given. It is given beyond explanation, and beyond human calculation. It is a gift completely beyond the range of human understanding, expectation, or explanation. It is God's own gift of the bread of life whereby God's own gift breaks the grip of the "bread of affliction."

A second text on such abundance beyond human imagination is the narrative moment in which Elisha and his servant are surrounded by the threatening army of the Syrian king (2 Kgs 6:8–23). Elisha's servant can count and can see that the two of them are outnumbered and endangered. But Elisha, a carrier of transformative power, knows otherwise; he bids his companion to see with different eyes. In his faith beyond what he could see, Elisha is able to reassure his servant: "Do not be afraid, for there are more with us than there are with them" (v. 16). A strange claim indeed! But when the servant receives new eyes, he saw: "The mountain was filled with horses and chariots of fire all around Elisha" (v. 17). The narrative explains nothing. It leaves us astonished by what is surely "beyond human imagination."

In both of these narratives concerning *bread from heaven* and *horses and chariots of fire*, the power of God is on exhibit that outruns human imagination. That power has an inexhaustible capacity for good gifts, never runs out, never lack resources, never ends in diminishment or in poverty. And that is because God's capacity is not situated in human scale. This is the God attested to Job, who has inexhaustible storehouses of resources and provisions that defy Job's arrogance (Job 38). This God of abundance is unlike any other. There is no one on the creaturely side of the equations—not Moses or Aaron in the wilderness, not Elisha or his servant under duress, and not Job in his consternation—who has such abundance. All others exhaust their capacity and deplete their abundance. But not God! God's abundance is beyond human explanation or expectation, more than we can ask or imagine!

When we consider the linkage of the claim for God "beyond imagination" to the economy, we intend to debunk the economics of scarcity that dominates our conventional imagination as it has been so compellingly advocated, for example, by Milton Friedman. That economics of scarcity has been eagerly committed to austerity and parsimony. As Mark Blyth, *Austerity: The History of a Dangerous Idea*, and Florian Schui, *Austerity: The Great Failure*, have shown, austerity is most often not an economic argument; it is rather a moral advocacy to make sure that the needy and the indigent (that is, the "undeserving") do not get something for nothing. As the recent Secretary of Agriculture, Sonny Purdue, has declared in roughly these words, "We don't want food stamps to make people dependent when they should be working." Stephanie Kelton, *The Deficit Myth: Modern Monetary Theory and the Birth of the People's Economy*, has shrewdly observed that the flaw in all such reasoning is the assumption that the budget of the federal government is like a family budget in which bills must be paid in order to base a better life on a balanced spreadsheet. The mistaken assumption is that the federal budget operates in the same way as a family budget. As a consequence, says Kelton,

> We have been too restrictive in public policy out of unwarranted fear about numbers recorded in the government agency spreadsheet. We have held back progress in science, fought unnecessary

wars, kept living standards low, and lived with less beauty than we could have enjoyed.[3]

In her very helpful study Kelton explains why the analogy to a family budget is not applicable. The qualitative difference between a family budget and the national government budget is that the federal government "makes money." Unlike a family budget it makes as much money as it needs, and it can never run out of money. For that reason "deficits" do not constitute a dangerous reality in the federal budget, a point made clear by the fact that the only people who ever worry about a deficit in the federal budget are those who want to stop specific actions. Thus not a "peep" was heard from Republicans concerning the Trump tax cut. Conversely, it is the same for Democrats who only worry about a deficit when Republicans are in charge. Nobody really defends "austerity" when it comes to one's own favorite projects; notably the defense budget always has a blank check for expenditure.

If we think about the government's capacity for abundance based on the capacity to "make money," we may suggest an analogue between the *limitless abundance of God* and the *limitless ability of the government to "make money,"* a capacity checked only by the threat of inflation. As God is unlike all creaturely abundance, there is no limit to God's abundance. As the federal government has no limit to the money it can make, it is unlike every other budgetary entity that is confined to the spreadsheet. Only God is limitless in abundance; only the federal government is limitless in making money. Kelton moreover, in an appeal to "Modern Monetary Theory," shows that well-planned, well administered deficits can add in transformative measures to the common life of the republic.

Kelton nicely draws the conclusion:

> Austerity is a *failure of imagination—a failure to imagine* how we can simultaneously improve living standards, invest in our nation's future, maintain a healthy economy, and manage inflation. Trade wars are a *failure of imagination—a failure to imagine* how we can simultaneously maintain domestic full employment, help poorer nations sustainably develop, lower our global carbon impact, and continue to enjoy the benefits from trade. Ecological exploitation is a *failure of imagination—a failure to imagine* how we can simultaneously improve living standards, maintain a prosperous

---

3. Kelton, *The Deficit Myth*, 260–61.

economy, and transition human activity so that we are protecting people and the planet.[4]

Kelton invites us to fresh imagination that is, as she says, nothing short of an analogue to the Copernican Revolution in which old assumptions are seen to be invalid and unhelpful for the reality that is in front of us. The reach of such a Copernican Revolution in our thinking about the economy seems to me closely linked to the imagery of "Kingdom of God" in the Bible, that is, an economy where the abundance of the creator God is the order of the day. This coming "Kingdom of God" is not an escape from history or from economy; it is rather a recalibration of history and economy that do not contradict the will and rule of the God of abundance. The prophetic texts teem with visions of such an abundance:

> They shall all sit under their own vines and under their own fig trees,
> and no one shall make them afraid. (Mic 4:4)

> Ho, everyone who thirsts,
>   come to the waters;
> and you that have no money,
>   come, buy and eat!
> Come, buy wine and milk
>   without money and without price. (Isa 55:1)

> I will summon the grain and make it abundant and lay no famine on you. I will make the fruit of the tree and the produce of the field abundant, so that you may never again suffer the disgrace of famine among the nations. (Ezek 36:29–30)

> The time is surely coming, says the LORD,
>   when the one who plows shall overtake the one who reaps,
>   and the treader of grapes the one who sows the seed;
> the mountains shall drip sweet wine,
>   and all the hills shall flow with it. (Amos 9:13)

And of course Jesus' performance of abundance with the bread is a reiteration of the manna story in which there are now baskets of surplus bread (Mark 6:30–44; 8:1–10).

All of these tests entail acts of daring imagination that function to "cancel" (!!) old assumptions and invite to new possibility. This Copernican Revolution is an act of imagination that summons us to see that all

---

4. Kelton, *The Deficit Myth*, 260–61; italics added.

of our old "spreadsheets" of balanced budgets are acts of fear and parsimony. And now fresh economic thinking permits us to be out beyond such spreadsheets.

Thus Kelton poses the question: "Can you imagine a people's economy?"[5] By her probe she means to envision an economy that is committed to common well-being in contrast to our present economy (and its assumptions) that are indifferent to common well-being and is ordered to serve only moneyed interests. She asks:

> Can you *imagine an economy* where private enterprise and public investment all combine to raise living standards for everyone?
>
> Can you *imagine an economy* where every rural and urban community has sufficient health, education, and transportation services to meet the needs of the local population?
>
> Can you *imagine an economy* that can measure and continually improve the human well-being, not just gross domestic product?
>
> Can you *imagine an economy* where human activity rejuvenates and enriches all ecosystems?
>
> Can you *imagine an economy* where nations trade in ways that enhance living standards and environmental conditions for all parties?
>
> Can you *imagine an economy* comprising a strong middle class with service- and labor-based occupations that have good wages and benefits?
>
> Can you *imagine an economy* where all are ensured a carefree retirement, with all their food, housing, and health-care needs met?
>
> Can you *imagine an economy* where all manner of research is fully funded, with a steady stream of successful ideas commercialized or rolled out to serve the public?[6]

Such acts of imagination are exactly the work of those who have signed on with the God of Abraham and have critical distance from present dominant imagination and freedom to move beyond a spreadsheet mentality.

We have ready at hand a familiar parable of the work of a people's economy in the film, *It's a Wonderful Life*.[7] The banker, Mr. Potter, is a full and compelling embodiment of *an economy of spreadsheets* that has no

---

5. Kelton, *The Deficit Myth*, 259.
6. Kelton, *The Deficit Myth*, 262–63; italics added.
7. Goodrich et al., screenwriters, *It's a Wonderful Life*.

interest in common well-being. The plot of the film is to show that a "people's economy" in neighborly generosity can rescue when the conventional economy of Mr. Potter has failed. The neighborhood, the film asserts, has adequate resources to redress the colossal error of Billy Bailey and to rescue George Bailey. The people's economy is subversive and transformative. The film, however, is not more than a parable because it operates at a micro-level. What is required now is the same people's economy at a macro-level for which the federal budget is at hand. Kelton shows the way in which such an economy might be organized on a national scale once the fear of the spreadsheet is overcome.

Kelton is clear that the alternative economy, justified in "Modern Monetary Theory," is an act of imagination. So let us be sober enough to recognize that there are not many venues for such dangerous subversive imagination in our society. The church (along with allied religious communities) is the only one left for such dangerous work. What if we recognize that the church community is exactly such a *zone for imagination* that breaks the grip of the spreadsheet? The church has the inscrutable text of Scripture that has always funded such alternative imagination. It has sacraments that perform before our very eyes the news of ample "bread of life" for abundance. It has proclamation of the news that the economy is under different management. The text, the sacrament, and the word may evoke a people's economy that may be generous, concrete, and neighborly. These acts of imagination expose our usual assumptions concerning economy are out of touch with human reality. It is impossible to "imagine" that Jesus intended anything less than the deployment of limitless resources of God's abundance for common wellbeing. Kelton concludes this way: "With the knowledge of how we can pay for it, it's now in your hands to imagine and to help build the people's economy."[8]

---

8. Kelton, *The Deficit Myth*, 263.

3

Bondage: Serve and Owe

THE PASSAGE OF THE "American Rescue Plan Act" has not only given accent to the crisis of the pandemic. It has also underscored the unbearable economic inequality between those left behind and those who have prospered through and benefitted from the pandemic. The energy around President Biden's plan has evoked for me attention to a remarkable, much neglected text that may indeed provide a clue to our economic recovery and well-being:

> For they are my servants whom I brought out of the land of Egypt;
> they shall not be sold as slaves are sold. (Lev 25:42)

This verse occurs near the end of a long chapter of regulations concerning the land and the economy. In every part of this regulation, (a) provision is made to protect the well-being of the land and a neighborly economy from unrestrained predation, and (b) care is taken to enact and ensure the intent of YHWH for the land and the people who belong to YHWH. In the specific paragraph of this verse, special protection is offered for those who become impoverished and go into debt (vv. 39–46). It is allowed that the ones indebted may be bound to their creditors, but only for a time, until the year of Jubilee. Thus the bondage of debt has clear, precise, and non-negotiable limitations, in order to prevent the formation of a permanent debtor class. It may be noted that in our verse, the terms rendered as "servants" and "slaves" are the same term, *'eved*. The two terms should both be translated in the same way, "slave" or "servant":

"my servants . . . not sold as servants," or

"my slaves . . . not sold as slaves."

The double rendering as "slaves" is in my judgment preferable, because that translation makes explicit reference to the slavery of Israel under Pharaoh, thus an allusion to the emancipation of the exodus. Thus the regulation asserts a limit to a predatory economy in which creditors enslave debtors to perpetuity.

The matter is immediately contemporary for us, because our economy readily preys upon those who remain hopelessly and forever in debt among us.

This regulation, together with its companion piece in Deut 15:1–18, constitutes the most explicit biblical teaching on the economy. The regulation of Deuteronomy 15 provides for the cancellation of debts in the seventh year, the "year of release." In this companion piece two verses are placed in startling juxtaposition. On the one hand,

> Since there will never cease to be some in need on the earth, I therefore command you, "Open your hand to the poor and needy neighbor in your land." (v. 11)

This is the verse famously quoted by Jesus:

> For you always have the poor with you, but you will not always have me. (Matt 26:11; see Mark 14:7)

Not so often noticed, on the other hand, is Deut 15:4:

> There will, however, be no one in need among you, because the LORD is sure to bless you in the land that the LORD your God is giving you as a possession to occupy.

In light of Deut 15:4, the observation of Matt 26:11 is not a statement of resignation. It is, rather, an observation that makes the practice of debt cancellation urgent. The statement of v. 4, moreover, ensures that if debt cancellation is regularly practiced, poverty can and will be eliminated. Thus the two verses must be read together. It is clear that the Torah provisions intend that the reality of YHWH's will pertains to the interruption and subversion of conventional economic practices whereby those with money (creditors) are free to use and exploit those without resources (debtors).

My attention has turned to this text in Lev 25:42 on two counts. First, I was reading *Scenes of Subjection: Terror, Slavery, and Self-Making*

BONDAGE: SERVE AND OWE

in Nineteenth-Century America by Saidiya V. Hartman that is a sobering, clear-eyed assessment of the import of US slavery and the long enduring wake of racism after emancipation. Hartman divides her analysis into two parts. In the first part concerning slavery, she studies slave "performances" that on the one hand served to amuse slave owners, but on the other hand at the same time were acts of defiance with the few tools the slaves had at their disposal.[1] Hartman pays particular attention to the practice of "stealing away," a phrase that referred to any momentary withdrawal from slave reality, even for worship, but that ultimately aimed at escape, emancipation, and abolition. This action of "stealing away to Jesus" is an exact echo of the request of the slaves in Egypt: "Let my people go, so that they may worship me" (Exod 8:20; see 10:3, 7). Worth noting is that the term "worship" is *'eved*, "serve," the same word used in Lev 25:32, "servant, slave." Thus worship equals "serve," so that worship is a dangerous, daring act of subversion, contradicting their servitude to Pharaoh. Hartman cites a case in which slaves had such a "praise meeting" that was overwhelmingly focused on freedom:

> When the patrollers discovered such meetings they would beat the slaves mercilessly in order to keep them from serving God. Turner recounted the words of one patroller to this effect: "If I ketch you here servin' God, I'll beat you. You ain't got no time to serve God. We bought you to serve us." Serving God was a crucial site of struggle, as it concerned issues about styles of worship, the intent of worship, and, most important, the very meaning of service, since the expression of faith was invariably a critique of the social conditions of subordination, servitude, and mastery. As Turner's account documents, the threat embodied in serving God was that the recognition of divine authority superseded, if not negated, the mastery of the slave owner.[2]

It is clear that any act of "stealing away" was a performance of the claim of God in Lev 25:42. The slaves in the US did not belong to white masters, but to the God of freedom, an affirmation that made slavery theologically illegitimate because such servitude preempted God's own claim. Thus slavery constituted a contest between the claim of God and claim of the slave system, a contest decisively settled in our verse. Hartman draws the stark

---

1. See also Scott, *Weapons of the Weak*.
2. Hartman, *Scenes of Subjection*, 66.

conclusion: "Serving God ultimately was to be actualized in the abolition of slavery.³

The second part of Hartman's book is an acute reflection on the status of ex-slaves in the post-emancipation economy. In the wake of emancipation, state governments operated by former slave owners were quick to enact Black Codes whereby ex-slaves were now bondaged in debt and were left economically bereft and hopeless in a system that fashioned new forms of servitude:

> Emancipation instituted indebtedness. Debt was at the center of a moral economy of submission and servitude and was instrumental in the production of peonage. Above all, it operated to bind the subject by compounding the service owed, augmenting the deficit through interest accrued, and advancing credit that extended interminably the obligation of service. The emancipated were introduced to the circuit of exchange through the figurative deployment of debt, which obliged them to both enter coercive contractual relationships and faithfully renumerate the treasure expended on their behalf. Furthermore, debt literally sanctioned bondage and propelled the freed toward indentured servitude by the selling off of future labor.⁴

Thus in Hartman's exposition the two historical periods are summarized:

Slavery: servitude;

Emancipation: debt.

Both periods feature bondage in which white control was beyond question or challenge. It is clear that our text in Lev 25:42 pertains exactly to these two conditions; on the one hand, endless servitude and on the other, brutal debt.

It is of course important that the brutalizing realities of slavery and Jim Crow be kept alive and available in our awareness. It is equally important, however, to see that the issues of servitude and debt are not only of long ago pertinence, but are present time contemporary social realities. A happy recent happenstance in my life is that my wife, Tia, and I discovered we were reading complementary books. Tia was reading a most important recent book, *The Sum of Us: What Racism Costs Everyone and How We Can Prosper Together* by Heather McGhee. At the same time I was reading

---

3. Hartman, *Scenes of Subjection*, 67.
4. Hartman, *Scenes of Subjection*, 131.

Makers and Takers: The Rise of Finance and the Fall of American Business by Rana Foroohar. It is not often that our reading converges as it did in this case. The book by McGhee narrates with acute critical awareness the brutal, costly reality of racism among us. At the same time, Foroohar provides important data about our current economic reality. The thesis of her book is that "finance" has come to dominate our economy to the severe detriment of business and manufacturing. By "finance," Foroohar refers to the fact that major corporations that used to "make" things have found it more profitable (lucrative!) to engage in credit, loans, and debt on a huge scale than it is to do their ordinary business. Surprisingly enough, this includes such companies as GM, GE, and Apple. The practice of "finance" produces immediate economic gains for shareholders. It also preys upon the vulnerable who finally may end in an ocean of debt. Thus, for example, the hustle of sub-prime loans that eventuated in the severe recession of 2008 was a strategy (scheme!) whereby vulnerable people were placed in hopeless debt and lost everything. See the summary of that strategy by Aaron Glantz, *Homewreckers: How a Gang of Wall Street Kingpins, Hedge Fund Magnates, Crooked Banks, and Venture Capitalists Suckered Millions Out of Their Homes and Demolished the American Dream.* Among those indicted by Glantz is Donald Trump who colluded with his buddy, Sean Hannity. Foroohar's verdict goes this way:

> With the rise of the securities and trading portion of the industry came a rise in debt of all kinds, public and private. Debt is the life-blood of finance; it is where the financial industry makes its money . . . Finance . . . has, perversely, all but ensured that debt is indispensable to maintaining any growth at all in an advanced economy like the United States, where 70 percent of output is consumer spending.[5]

We may consider both *the slavery-Jim Crow reality of servitude and debt* and the *contemporary force of finance* that reduces to debt and dependency not unlike servitude in the contestation with Lev 25:42. I suggest that this interface of *slavery–Jim Crow* and *contemporary "finance"* with Lev 25:42 yields two questions that may preoccupy us:

Who serves whom?

Who owes what to whom?

---

5. Foroohar, *Makers and Takers*, 9.

These two questions concern servitude and debt. "Debt" is the leverage that the moneyed class exercises on order to maintain a dependable labor pool, an exercise that of course extends to immense student debt that requires and ensures regular long-term work. Such debt has become definitional for our economy, ensuring that the defining relationships among us are those between creditor and debtor. The requirements of the present arrangement are less dramatic than those of the nineteenth century of servitude and indentured debt. It is easy enough, however, to show that the same leverage works that operates now as it did then, the leverage of servitude and debt.

I suggest that we might well focus on these two questions:

- Who serves whom?
- Who owes what to whom?

Of course for many in the churches of the moneyed class there is no servitude and no significant debt. But then we must ask in any case, *How is it that we may participate beneficially in a system that aggressively produces debt and servitude?*

The "news" from Moses and the Torah is that the God of covenantal emancipation does not intend debilitating or immobilizing servitude. The God of covenantal emancipation intends that economic life will be ordered to preclude such ways of bondage. If and when we focus on these two questions, we have an opportunity to grasp afresh the core intent of the gospel. So much of our attention and energy have been siphoned off into private salvation, escapist spirituality, and otherworldliness. But the verdict of Lev 25:42 tells otherwise. It is this claim for the God of covenantal emancipation that sets in motion the exodus narrative, the mandates of Sinai, and the prophetic insistence on alternative. And if that were not enough, we imagine a nearly straight line that runs from Lev 25:42 to the dictum of Jesus:

> No one can serve two masters; for a slave will either hate the one and love the other, or be devoted to the one and despise the other. You cannot serve God and wealth. (Matt 6:24; Luke 16:13)

(We have nicely taken the sting out of this sharp either/or by conventionally translating the second element of the last sentence as "mammon," a word not readily understood among us. More recent translations have boldly used the term "wealth" that makes the saying much more pointed and demanding.) In Matthew this dictum is followed by Jesus' invitation to move beyond anxiety about "things" for a life toward God's kingdom, a life delivered from anxiety about food, drink, or clothing, that is, a life free from covetous fear and greed (Matt 6:5–33). The same dictum in Luke follows Jesus' parable of worldly advice about dishonest wealth and the offer of true riches (Luke 16:1–9).

There is a compelling expectation that this trajectory of teaching that runs from Leviticus to the teaching of Jesus can refocus our understanding of the gospel and our practice of faith. It turns out, in this trajectory, that the gospel is all about *whom to serve* and *what to owe*. While these matters are open to theological dimension, their accent is on the reality of our material life. This trajectory constitutes an invitation (summons?) to the pastors, teachers, and interpreters of the church to give primary attention to servitude and debt, and the way in which these destructive practices continue to skew the real life of the world. An economy based on servitude clearly does not serve the coming kingdom of God but has chosen wealth rather than God. An economy based on debt likewise has chosen wealth rather than God. In a season of servitude, what is required is emancipation, exactly the work and will of the exodus God. In a society of debt what is required is cancellation of debt, exactly the intent of the Jubilee year and the "year of release."

It is something of a surprise to find that our lead text occurs in the book of Leviticus. It is a surprise because the book of Leviticus is primarily concerned with God's holiness and the essential safeguards that may protect that holiness. But then in the mandates of Leviticus 19 we get commandments concerning the poor (vv. 9–10) and the neighbor (vv. 17–18). It turns out that God's holiness is not simply a cultic affair or a religious phenomenon. God's holiness, in biblical horizon, is other than that because this God is relentlessly committed to the neighborhood; for that reason holiness tilts toward covenantal neighborly justice. This reality serves as a corrective to the more popular notion of holiness as famously articulated by Rudolf Otto,[6] who understood holiness as the awesome experience of the "numinous." Walter Kaiser sees that for Otto, holiness is an "affective experience, not one anchored in the character of God." But the Bible to the contrary, and especially Leviticus 19,

> insists that faith and ethics are necessary aspects of the same coin, though they are by no means identical. Faith must demonstrate its

---

6. Otto, *The Idea of the Holy*.

authenticity by the way it operates in the ordinary affairs of life. The religious life of faith must have ethical outcomes if it makes a claim to authenticity.[7]

The historical review of McGhee concerning the continuing brutality of racism and the analysis of contemporary "finance" by Foroohar together attest to the practice of bondage, ancient and contemporary, that violates the holiness of God and that transgresses the requirements of neighborliness. Wealth as the ultimate goal of a slave economy, and wealth as the ultimate goal of contemporary "finance" in every case make life "nasty, brutal, and short." The gospel attests to an alternative. That alternative requires emancipation from servitude and cancelation of immobilizing debt. The God of Moses and of Jesus intends otherwise, nothing less than "life abundant." But "life abundant" requires emancipation and cancelation of debt. It turns out that these requirements are as urgent and as contemporary as the "American Rescue Plan Act." More than that plan is required. Nonetheless that plan may provide entry into fresh exploration of the claims of faith, the reality of the holy one, and the needs of the neighborhood. The plan may hint at a wake-up call from a season when wealth and finance, servitude and debt seemed normal. Entrusted to us is responsibility for a very different normalcy that awaits implementation.

---

7. Kaiser, *Book of Leviticus*, 1131–32.

4

Borne Away

AT AGE 87, I think about death only occasionally. By the witness of our local paper in its obituaries, many people live a very long life in northern Michigan. So there is that. What drew me back to the hymn I consider here was witnessing Donald Trump's desperate flight to Mar-a-Lago from DC. His shame-filled departure recalled to me a line for Isaac Watts's great hymn, "O God Our Help in Ages Past." (In the new Presbyterian hymnal, *Glory to God*, the phrase is altered to "Our God Our Help in Ages Past," thus linking the singing church more closely and intimately to the wondrous long-term sovereignty of God.)

Watts's hymn concerns the reality of death and the reliable governance of God beyond the reality of death. I have found the fifth stanza to be pertinent to the pitiful departure of Trump:

> Time like an ever rolling stream,
> bears all its sons away;
> they fly forgotten, as a dream
> dies at the opening day.[8]

In order to avoid male language it has changed "all its sons" to "all our years," a much less poignant rendering. Rather than such an anemic translation we might sing "bears us all away.") You cannot beat the roll of time. And so Trump departed. He will leave serious wounds among us, but the passage of time, maybe a long time, assures that he will have been a bad dream, a dream that dies at sunrise.

8. *Glory to God*, 687.

While the hymn plays upon Psalm 90, this particular verse referred me, first of all, to Psalm 73. In that Psalm "the wicked" are characterized as uncaring in their wealth and cynical self-indulgence. The wicked are attractive to the Psalmist who envies them:

> But as for me, my feet had almost stumbled;
>   my steps had nearly slipped.
> For I was envious of the arrogant;
>   I saw the prosperity of the wicked. (Ps 73:2–3)

But then the Psalmist comes to her senses and recognizes the uncompromising moral reality of life in God's world:

> Until I went into the sanctuary of God;
>   Then I perceived their end. (v. 17)

The Psalmist saw that for all of attractive self-indulgence of the wicked, in the long run of God's governance, such a life is unsustainable, has no staying power, and so has no lasting significance. As a consequence, the Psalmist anticipates the risk and destiny of the indulgent rich whom he had envied:

> Truly you set them in slippery places;
>   you make them fall to ruin.
> How they are destroyed in a moment,
>   swept away utterly by terrors!
> They are like a dream when one awakes;
>   on awakening you despise their phantoms. (vv. 18–20)

They are bound to fail and to fall to ruin, because God has ordered the world otherwise. Verse 19 voices two strong verbs concerning their demise, "destroyed" and "utterly swept away." Finally they are only despised. The Psalmist, like Watts, uses the word "dream" to mark the unreality of such a life. Watts has them "forgotten"; the Psalmist has them "despised." Either way, they are gone!

But of course the hymn, unlike Psalm 73, does not make a moral distinction concerning the "wicked" or the "righteous." In the hymn, not only will the wicked be utterly swept away. All of us, every one of us, will be borne away. Thus even if President Biden does real well with his recovery program, as we may hope and expect, he too will be borne away as will all those who support him and those who oppose him. The "rolling stream" of time is a great leveler, indifferent as it is to our moral distinctions. The wicked and the righteous face the same ending because the ever rolling stream of time is indiscriminate:

> All this I laid to heart, examining it all, how the righteous and the wise and their deeds are in the hand of God; whether it is love or hate one does not know. Everything that confronts them is vanity, since the same fate comes to all, to the righteous and the wicked, to the good and evil, to the clean and the unclean, to those who sacrifice and those who do not sacrifice. As are the good, so are the sinners; those who swear are like those who shun an oath. This is an evil in all that happens under the sun, that the same fate comes to everyone. (Eccl 9:1–3)

The same sober recognition of reality is voiced in Psalm 90 which has guided and funded Watts in the articulation of his hymn.

> You sweep them [morals] away; they are like a dream,
>   like grass that is renewed in the morning;
> in the morning it flourishes and is renewed;
>   in the evening it fades and withers . . .
> The days of our life are seventy years,
>   or perhaps eighty, if we are strong;
> even then their span is only toil and trouble;
>   they are soon gone, and we fly away. (Ps 90:1–6, 10)

In juxtaposing the verdict of Psalm 73 and the large vision of an ending in Psalm 90 and echoed by Watts, I have puzzled. On the one hand, in Psalm 73 the wicked are wept way. On the other hand, in Psalm 90 all are swept away, without moral distinction. The simple solution is to recognize that different Psalms are pertinent to different folk in different circumstances. When we take the long vision of Psalm 90 with Watts, we can recognize that our moral distinctions do not count for much. The Psalmist imagines that we all, without distinction, stand before a mighty shared wrath (Ps 90:7–9).

Such a conclusion might lead to resignation or to indifference. None of it matters anyway! Such a conclusion might be drawn by the cynically self-indulgent featured in Psalm 73 and by those tempted to self-centeredness:

> Fools say in their hearts,
>   "There is no God."
> They are corrupt,
>   they do abominable deeds;
>   there is no one who does good! (Ps 14:1)

That, however, is not the judgment reached in the long history of faith. In that long history of faith, the faithful have always found that there are special occasions amid the ever flowing stream of time that are freighted with both summons and opportunity. For such freighted times, we have the urgency-noting term *kairos*. These are moments of time that are laden with urgent summons and opportunity to which the faithful may respond in eager obedience and glad investment.

Thus even in the face of the ever-rolling stream that in the end leaves us all exposed, the faithful readily muster attentiveness and energy in order to engage in a performance of God's intention for which the biblical word is "kingdom." The Bible attests that the faithful are "all in" for that moment, without regard for being borne away. It is a primary mark of faith not only to yield in trust to God's ever "rolling stream," but to engage in laden moments when the will and goodness of God surge among us in peculiarly overwhelming ways.

While Psalm 90 with its wistfulness is "a prayer of Moses," the narrative of the Exodus shows that Moses was "all in" with emancipation, even in the face of the dangerous presence of Pharaoh. Isaiah, even though he knew of the huge trouble coming to his people and city (Isa 6:9–13), was all in: "Here am I, send me" (6:8). And of course the gospel narratives tell us of the way in which the summons to "Follow me" on the lips of Jesus evoked a response of "immediately" from the disciples who were all in with his call (Mark 1:17–18). None of this immediacy and urgency can override the continuing force of the ever-flowing stream. But the faithful engage in no transcendent escape. The faithful, rather, trust the ultimacy of the rule of God and give their lives over to the *kairotic* moment in front of them. Thus, I suggest, is the wondrous difference between the faithful who will be borne away, and the cynically self-indulgent, also borne away who never notice such *kairotic* moments.

This double reality of *the long term of faith-cum-death* and *the immediacy of kairos* offers us a useful double vision. My impression is that the church is much better on *the long term* than on the *immediacy of kairos*. It is better on the long term, perhaps because the church a regular venue for funerals. That is something we do well and we are, in any congregation, regularly reminded of our mortality and the truth of our death. Or perhaps better because such an accent gives us a chance to witness to the abiding sovereignty of God's gracious compassion. Indeed, the Psalmist counts on that compassion and makes a bid for it:

> Have compassion on your servants!
> Satisfy us in the morning with your steadfast love,
>   so that we may rejoice and be glad all our days.
> Make us glad as many days as you have afflicted us,
>   and as many years as have seen evil. (Ps 90:13b–15)

The church, it strikes me, is not nearly as good in a consistent way about the *kairotic moments* that are thrust on us that demand of us that we turn our energy and attentiveness away from the long term to the immediacy in front of us. The testimony of faith is that those who engage that turn are willing and able for the moment to leave the long term to God, and to "bet it all" on this moment. The saints whom we celebrate were, in every case, "all in" to a *kairotic moment* without any regard for being "borne away."

I judge that we are now, in the US church, at exactly such a moment that invites our attention away from the long term to focus on this moment in which the kingdom of God is crowding in on us and summoning us to sign on. The signs of the *kairos* are all around us:

- the end of patriarchy and the empowerment of women;
- the fresh awareness that "Black lives matter," and so an urgent redress of old habits of systemic racism;
- the urgent recognition that poor people are among us with a requirement of security and dignity, and so a reordering of the policies and structures that evoke and sustain long-term poverty;
- the emancipation, empowerment, and dignity of those who violate old sexual norms for the sake of healthy wellbeing;
- the healing of creation that cries out in its long term woundedness.

The list can be extended and is familiar to us. All of these components (and others to be added) are all of a piece and together attest long term alienation from the will and purpose of the creator God. This is a moment when the emergence of the Kingdom of God comes upon us with a compelling immediacy.

I am, finally, drawn to the ending of Psalm 90. After the Psalmist bids for God's compassion (v. 13), the Psalm ends with another petition:

> Prosper the work of our hands—
>   O prosper the work of our hands! (v. 17)

This prayer is a recognition in the faithful that their work matters, they have done something that is noted in God's purview. What they have done now receives the affirmation and guarantee of God in order that it might endure. That petition is one that the "wicked" in Psalm 73 cannot utter. The wicked have no "work of their hands" that might endure or that might receive the guarantee of God; they have done nothing. They have shared nothing. They have given nothing. They have done nothing that coheres with God's coming rule. Unlike those in Psalm 73, the faithful in Psalm 90 may pray in boldness and in hope that their work may continue to prosper. They, along with the wicked, are sure to be borne away by the ever "rolling stream" of time. But they have the assurance (that allows peaceableness) that their work coheres with "your work" (Ps 90:16). They are not forgotten, not a nightmare, more than a dream, kept in compassion. Even while borne away, the voice of faith in Psalm 73 can still hope:

> Nevertheless, I am continually with you;
>   you hold my right hand.
> You guide me with your counsel,
>   and afterward you will receive me with honor.
> Whom have I in heaven but you?
>   And there is nothing on earth that I desire other than you.
> My flesh and my heart may fail,
>   but God is the strength of my heart and my portion forever.
> (Ps 73:23–26)

5

Discriminatory Gaslighting

I WATCHED THE INTERVIEW of Meghan Markle and Prince Harry by Oprah Winfrey. I read about the reaction of the royal family to the interview in which members of the royal family attempted to undermine or deconstruct the memory of Harry and Meghan about how they had been treated. And then I learned what was for me a new phrase, "discriminatory gaslighting," as it has been exposited by Christy Pichichero, "Meghan and Harry Experienced Discriminatory Gaslighting: Here's How You Can Tell." The term "gaslighting" is a new phrase to me:

> Consolidating one's power by causing individuals to question their own judgments, perceptions of reality and memories, has a name: gaslighting. It is a form of psychological manipulation by which abusers build their authority—and ability to continue to abuse— by breaking down their victim's or victims' sense of self and their confidence in their grip on reality.[1]

It is easy enough to say that,

> The victim misunderstood a decision, misjudged a gesture, or behavior, or misinterpreted someone's words ("recollections may vary").

The modifying word, "discriminatory," simply means that the gaslighter, for any number of reasons, may claim high ground and become condescending toward or dismissive of the one gaslighted. All of this was clearly operative in the royal response to the interview. The effect is to

---

1. Pichichero, "Meghan and Harry."

undermine the self-confidence of the ones critiqued in order to make them more dependent upon the authority and generosity of the gaslighter. So I have a new word for what is an obvious effort in the case of Meghan and Harry, and in many other cases as well. Clear enough!

In the wake of my new learning, it is perhaps useful to reflect on the practice of gaslighting; as our politics becomes less and less principled and more and more aggressively partisan and destructive, we might be alert to the ways in which the biblical tradition witnesses to such a practice. So here is a list of scripture references I could think of in which someone or some group is victimized or blamed in ways that challenge their social significance or social function and seeks to dismiss such persons or groups as socially unacceptable or irrelevant.

In the exodus narrative, Pharaoh continues to increase the production schedule for bricks made by Hebrew slaves. When the slaves protest Pharaoh's aggressive imposition, Pharaoh responds: "You are lazy, lazy" (Exod 5:17; see v. 8). This "verdict" on the lips of Pharaoh, intensified by the doubled term, is designed to focus on the failure of the brick production by the slaves, and to divert attention away from Pharaoh's predatory greed. If his verdict can be made to stick, then Pharaoh's verdict will become definitional for the slaves, will protect Pharaoh from criticism, and will mandate the slaves to even more intense productivity. The gaslighting is so that the slaves may perceive their life and role solely on Pharaoh's terms. In this instance, the verdict did not and could not stick, because of the emancipatory intervention of YHWH that exposed Pharaoh's gaslighting as phony and without substance. It is YHWH,

> who struck Egypt through their firstborn,
>   for his steadfast love endures forever;
> and brought Israel out from among them,
>   for his steadfast love endures forever;
> with a strong hand and an outstretched arm,
>   for his steadfast love endures forever;
> who divided the Red Sea in two,
>   for his steadfast love endures forever;
> and made Israel pass through the midst of it,
>   for his steadfast love endures forever;
> but overthrew Pharaoh and his army in the Red Sea,
>   for his steadfast love endures forever. (Ps 136:10–15)

In this instance YHWH's steadfast love (tenacious solidarity) vetoed Pharaoh's gaslighting.

Discriminatory Gaslighting

This dismissive trope of Pharaoh of course permeates US history. The same verdict on white lips has gaslighted Black identity: "Colored people are lazy." And when they are lazy, it is evident that they are not bright, and therefore cannot manage their own lives but require paternalistic care. Thus the Pharaonic verdict has served white control and white imagination, and justified white supremacy. That comfortable white verdict has sheltered whites from recognition of the brutality toward and greedy exploitation of Black people, and has required Black people to accept life on white terms. Except of course we know better. We know that Black people, in their "hidden transcripts" have never accepted that white verdict and have resisted as they have been able to do.[2] White gaslighting of course continues even now in a fairly straight line from Pharaoh. It is only Pharaonic illusion that can take the verdict to be persuasive.

Great efforts at gaslighting are evident in the biblical text that attempt to discredit the prophets who are rightly seen as threats to the status quo in Israel. The prophets are uncredentialed voices, so that it was (and is) always easy to be dismissive of their dangerous presence. From the outset, Elisha was seen to be a threat to the sociopolitical status quo in Northern Israel. His work did not take long to evoke resistant hostility. In the odd narrative of 2 Kgs 2:23–25, Elisha is assaulted by a gang of young boys. They jeer at him concerning his bald head. The double use of "baldy" again shows the intensity with which the prophet is attacked. It may be that this jeering is innocent and only the silliness of young boys, a view taken by some commentators. But maybe not! The scene calls to my mind the aggressive jeering at the election board in Florida in 2000 urging that the vote count be stopped so that George W. Bush would be elected president. The loud jeering looked on TV like the spontaneous action of young enthusiastic males. It turned out, however, that the young men making the loud scene on TV were paid performers for the Republican Party. Such a scene in our own day allows me to think that the young boys mocking the bald prophet may have been dispatched by their elders who hoped by this mockery to discredit the prophet. The gaslighting of Elisha is because his appearance does not "measure up." The prophet of course remains unintimidated by the jeering. Thus his curse of the boys evokes two she-bears who savagely stop the gaslighting of the prophet (v. 24). The prophet will not and need not succumb to such an assault.

---

2. See Scott, *Weapons of the Weak*; and Scott, *Domination and the Arts of Resistance*.

Lament That Generates Covenant

A similar attempt at gaslighting concerns the prophet Hosea who likewise is perceived as a threat to dominant society. The threat voiced by the prophet is countered by what may have been a popular form of gaslighting, the kind that now is phoned in to talk radio. We are not told who speaks the gaslighting here. The dismissal of Hosea is in two parallel lines:

> The prophet is a fool,
> the man of the spirit is mad. (Hos 9:7)

On the one hand, a "fool" is one who is out of touch with reality; on the other hand, a *meshuga*, a crazy man. Who but a fool would say such outrageous things as Hosea is saying? Who but a crazy person would dare to assault the time-honored institutions of society? And because he is a crazy fool, no attention should be paid to him. This same gaslighting verdict is likely to be to be conveniently reiterated concerning anyone who speaks beyond accepted social reality.

This dismissive verdict concerning Hosea is readily paired with a dismissive verdict against Jeremiah who has so much in common with Hosea. Jeremiah's primary theme in the book of Jeremiah is that Jerusalem will be destroyed by Babylon; more than that, this destruction of Jerusalem is the will of YHWH. In this reading of history, obedience to YHWH amounts to a willing surrender to Babylon. That counsel in the midst of the military crisis faced by Jerusalem is enough to evoke the active hostility of Jerusalem "officials." The officials brought Jeremiah before King Zedekiah with a verdict already clear in their minds:

> This man ought to be put to death, because he is discouraging the soldiers who are left in the city, and all the people by speaking such words to them. For this man is not seeking the welfare of his people, but their harm. (Jer 38:4)

The Hebrew has it, Jeremiah is "weakening the hands" of the soldiers; that is, he is undermining the war effort. (This accusation has been echoed many times, for example, in the case of Eugene Debs, who was imprisoned [1918–1921] for his opposition to World War I.) Amid the fever of war, those who sponsor or support or benefit from the war effort are characteristically vigilant against any who think otherwise. Jeremiah was an outspoken critic of popular opinion that supported resistance to Babylon, a resistance that in the long run was sure to fail. What the supporters of the war could not tolerate was Jeremiah's expansive version of YHWH's governance that included Babylon as well as Israel that thereby compromised the easy "chosenness" imagined in Jerusalem. In this case the prophet was rescued by a eunuch in the royal palace (38:7–13). Subsequently he was captured and eventually carried off, against his will, to Egypt (see 43:1–7). Even in Egypt against his will, however, Jeremiah refused to be silenced. He anticipated that Babylon, with its strong (he would have said "God-given") military capacity, would wreak havoc even in Egypt:

> Thus says the Lord of hosts, the God of Israel. I am going to send and take my servant King Nebuchadrezzar of Babylon and he will set his throne above these stones that I have buried, and he will spread his royal canopy over them. He shall come and ravage the land of Egypt. (vv. 10–11)

In his purview there was no place to hide from the reach of YHWH's governance, not even in far off Egypt.

These three instances concerning *Elisha, Hosea,* and *Jeremiah* together attest to the ways in which established ideology sought to fend off prophetic truth-telling. That ideology may be on the lips of young boys who have inhaled their parents' passion. The verdict may be "crazy" or "treason." (In the contemporary case of Jeremiah Wright, for example, I suppose we get a popular verdict against him that combines "crazy" and "traitor." The media and the political class determined that Wright had to be severely critiqued in the defense of the status quo that his inflammatory rhetoric so much threatened).

As I began to think about "discriminatory gaslighting," I was surprised to see that the rule of "clean, unclean" occurred everywhere in the biblical text to sort out those who are acceptable or unacceptable. Those unlike "us" who constitute a threat to a homogeneous normality are easily labeled as "unclean" or an "an abomination." A choice example of such exclusionary rhetoric is voiced by Ezra in his prayer. The exclusionary verdict is in the mouth of YHWH:

> The land that you are entering to possess is a land unclean with the pollutions of the peoples of the lands, with their abominations. They have filled it from end to end with their uncleanness. (Ezra 9:11)

Of course "unclean" has been a racist trope from the outset. Already in the Joseph narrative,

> They served him by himself, and them by themselves, and the Egyptians who ate with him by themselves, because the Egyptians

could not eat with the Hebrews, for that is an abomination to the Egyptians. (Gen 43:42)

(Not without reason was the first venture in the Civil Rights movement at "lunch counters," because eating together was judged an abomination!) The verdict "abomination" is a generic dismissal of those unable to qualify. And of course the verdict, "Colored people are unclean" is a way of racial exclusion from social acceptance. Richard Beck, *Unclean: Meditations on Purity, Hospitality, and Mortality,* himself an evangelical, offers a stunning inventory of what constitutes "unclean" in contemporary religious life. He lays out a helpful; taxonomy of five "moral foundations:

Harm/Care;

Fairness/Reciprocity;

Ingroup/Loyalty;

Authority/Respect; and

Purity/Sanctity.[3]

He concludes that religious conservatives have a much larger catalogue of "unclean" than do religious liberals:

> Liberals tend to restrict their normative judgments to the Harm/Care and the Fairness/Reciprocity foundations. That is, liberals will tend to cry "That's Wrong!" when someone is being *harmed/not-cared-for* or when something is *unfair/unjust*. Liberals don't, as a rule, often make appeals to the foundations of Ingroup/Loyalty, Authority/Respect, and Purity/Sanctity. Although liberals are not insensitive or unmoved by the warrants of Ingroup/Loyalty, Authority/Respect, and Purity/Sanctity, liberals appeal to these foundations much less frequently when compared to conservatives. By contrast, conservatives deploy all five foundations when they make normative judgments. This means that a much wider range of stimuli will offend conservatives.[4]

In his ministry, Jesus regularly defied and transgressed the conventions of clean and unclean. For that reason, surely, the vision of Peter in Acts 10 attests to an overthrow of the popular dominant categories of clean and unclean, in this case concerning Jews and Gentiles: "What God has made clean you must not call profane" (Acts 10:25).

3. Beck, *Unclean,* 58–59.
4. Beck, *Unclean,* 59–60.

Thus, an end to that particular form of gaslighting that has been operative in some forms of Judaism! Clearly gaslighting about uncleanness and impurity is no monopoly of Judaism, but has been much more virulent in some forms of Christianity. It is surely ironic that the immediate case of gaslighting with reference to Harry and Meghan turns, yet again, on the issue of race!

These five instances of *Pharaoh, Elisha, Hosea, Jeremiah,* and *Peter* are prominent efforts at social delegitimation by gaslighting:

Pharaoh: You are **lazy lazy!**

Forty-two young boys: **baldy, baldy!**

Popular judgment concerning Hosea; **fool, madman!**

Jerusalem officials concerning Jeremiah: **traitor!**

Religious authorities concerning many folk: **unclean!**

In each case the gaslighting is done by *established power* against those who are manifestly *powerless*. In each case the one attacked is perceived as a threat to the established order.

This evidence—that could surely be expanded—is enough to see that the primary trajectory of the Bible is on the side of those who are regularly gaslighted, and against those who gaslight in order to maintain power and status. In the end, this is what distinguishes the God of Israel—the God of the Gospel—from all other gods. Conventional gods are on the side of the status quo and are easily allied with such gaslighting. They rock no boats but legitimate established human power. The God of the gospel, to the contrary, shows up otherwise.

This God shows up in the slave camps of Egypt;

This God shows up in the transformative narratives of Elisha;

This God shows up in the subversive utterance of Hosea;

This God shows up in the large vista of sovereignty voiced by Jeremiah;

This God shows up among those now declared to be clean.

This conclusion is, to be sure, a version of the liberation signature: "God's preferential option for the poor." It is a recognition that the God of the gospel is not inured in the religious or secular version of established truth. In all these cases I have cited, the truth enacted is not impressed by or deterred by gaslighting, even in its boldly discriminatory forms. It is the work of truth-telling to debunk the gaslighting that serves only to sanction privilege and advantage when they are under threat from below.

This trajectory of truth-telling from below culminates, for Christians, in Jesus of Nazareth. Of course Jesus, in his refusal of all gaslighting, posed an unbearable threat to established order. Terry Eagleton summarizes:

> The morality Jesus preaches is reckless, extravagant, improvident, over-the-top, a scandal to actuaries and a stumbling block to real estate agents; forgive your enemies, give away your cloak as well as your coat, turn the other cheek, love those who insult you, walk the extra mile, take no thought for tomorrow.[5]

No wonder this trajectory of truth-telling perennially constitutes such a threat to treasured socioeconomic arrangements. No wonder, moreover, that human agents situated in this trajectory, in its many articulations, draw to themselves these various gaslighting efforts such as "lazy, baldy, crazy, traitor, or unclean." No wonder indeed!

---

5. Eagleton, *Reason, Faith, and Revolution*, 14

6

Lament that Generates Covenant

IN THE MID-FIFTH CENTURY BCE (about 450 BCE), exiled Jews in Babylon made their way home after their displacement. They were led home by Ezra the scribe and Nehemiah the governor. When they arrived back in Jerusalem, they found a sorry situation of stress and economic distress. Ezra the scribe, in response to their new sorry circumstance, voiced a long prayer (Neh 9:6–37). The prayer touches all the normal bases of conventional prayer including praise and thanksgiving to God for mercy, and confession of sin. The prayer ends in petition and lament. The petition is a bid that God should pay attention to their dire straits:

> Do not treat lightly all the hardship that has come upon us, our kings, our officials, our priests, our prophets, our ancestors, and all your people, since the time of the kings of Assyria until today. (v. 32)

The prayer ends with the most pathos-filled of all biblical laments:

> Here we are, slaves to this day—slaves in the land that you gave to our ancestors to enjoy is fruit and it good gifts. Its rich yield goes to the kings whom you have set over us because of our sins; they have power also over our bodies and over our livestock at their pleasure, and we are in great distress. (vv. 36–37)

The prayer lines out for God the dreadful economic condition of the returned Jews. All of their produce is severely taxed by the Persians ("those over us"). It is the Persians who enjoy the good produce of the land of promise. No wonder the lament concludes, "We are in great distress." They

Lament That Generates Covenant

are in such great distress that Ezra cannot even muster a good loud demanding imperative to God. The ending of the prayer is more like a helpless whimper.

In context, however, we can see that even this prayer of lament is not without generative force:

- the lament allows Israel to identify properly its true circumstance without illusion;
- the lament permits Israel to disengage from the ideological hegemony of the Persians;
- the lament allows the returnees to engage in depth with their tradition of faith concerning the God of mercy;
- the lament invites them to a sense of community amid their suffering; and
- the lament authorizes the mustering emotive energy for what has to be done for a viable future.

There is no evidence that God answered the prayer. There is, however, compelling evidence that those who prayed honestly were empowered to act for the sake of a new future.

In the next paragraph it is reported that they made a new covenantal agreement for the sake of organizing community power and faith as a community alternative to the Persian hegemony. The new agreement included:

- provision for Sabbath, an assurance that common life would not be reduced to commerce and commodity (Neh 10:31a);
- a provision for debt relief every seven years (as in the Torah provision), thus supplying relief from economic deprivation (10:31b);
- a series of different offerings that no doubt contributed to the common good (10:32–39).

This new covenant was surely evoked and empowered by the truth-telling of the lament. It turns out that the lament of Ezra was not an act of resignation, but an act of new resolve. The public voicing of grief may lead to new social energy. My hunch is that every stirring of emancipatory power among the powerless begins in lament. Where there is no lament, there can only be violence. Where there is vigorous lament, new social energy is released. Ezra's prayer set in motion new social possibility!

7

Majoring in Minors[1]

IN THE MIDST OF the pandemic, Fareed Zakaria, a well-known journalist and commentator, has published a short accessible book titled, *Ten Lessons for a Post-Pandemic World*. In one of his chapters Zakaria has this "lesson": "The world is digital." This "lesson" leads Zakaria to explore the current technological revolution and the expansive reach of Artificial Intelligence. At the end of his chapter he draws an important conclusion:

> The smarter a machine becomes at calculating data and providing answers, the more it forces us to think about what is uniquely human about us, beyond our ability to reason. In fact, intelligent machines might make us prize our human companions even more, for their creativity, whimsy, unpredictability, warmth, and intimacy.[2]

Given his recognition that advanced and advancing technology increasingly takes over human functions, Zakaria ends his commentary in this way:

> For much of history, humans were praised for many qualities other than their power to calculate—bravery, loyalty, generosity, faith, love. The movement to digital life is broad and fast and real. But perhaps one of its deepest consequences will be to make us cherish the things in us that are most human.[3]

---

1. I am glad to borrow this title phrase from Boring, *Gospel of Matthew*, 435, in his exposition of Matt 23:23–24.
2. Zakaria, *Ten Lessons*, 121.
3. Zakaria, *Ten Lessons*, 121.

My hunch is that Zakaria did not spend great energy in articulating his inventory of things human: bravery, loyalty, generosity, faith, love. But it is an inventory that might occur to many of us. His list is an invitation to think further about the singular capacity and distinctive responsibilities that belong to our humanness. It is possible, given the world that technology makes available to us, that we become thoughtless, careless or indifferent about the distinctively human and expend our energy and attention on less noble or less appropriate matters. That is, we might confuse what is urgent for us as human beings and what are more convenient and easier targets of satisfaction that may claim our energy and attention.

Because Zakaria has set up the problem in this way—the *distinctively human* and *everything else*—I am drawn to the recital of "woes" in the gospel of Matthew that Jesus articulates against the scribes, Pharisees, and hypocrites, the ones who distort the claims of faith for advantage in the world (Matt 23:13–36). Specifically, my attention turned to vv. 23–24 in which Jesus sees that his opponents had focused on lesser matters and neglected the primary claims of faith:

> Woe to you scribes and Pharisees, hypocrites! For you tithe *mint, dill and cumin*, and neglect the weightier matters of the law: *justice and mercy and faith*. It is these you ought to have practiced without neglecting the others. You blind guides! You strain out a gnat but swallow a camel! (vv. 23–24)

The same distortion is noted in the tradition of cleanness and purity in Matt 15:1–20 (see Mark 7:1–23). In both Matthew 15 and our text in Matthew 23, Jesus critiques an excessive punctiliousness about relatively minor matters while the big claims of faith are lost. Thus I suggest that the big claims of faith in the gospel are akin to the human qualities noted by Zakaria. As technology crowds human qualities, so distorted punctiliousness detracts from the big claims of faith.

Given that distraction and distortion by expansive technology, the pastors, teachers, and interpreters of the church have an urgent responsibility to accent the big claims of faith at which Zakaria hints in his chapter. In these strictures of Jesus, these big claims are *justice, mercy,* and *faith* (*krisis, eleos, pistis*). This triad focuses attention on human interactions that are generative of common well-being. We may notice much the same affirmation of human interaction in the familiar triad of Paul, "*faith, hope, and love*" (*pistis, elpis, agapē*) (1 Cor 13:13).

There is no doubt that that this triad of *justice, mercy, and faith* on the lips of Jesus is derived from Israel's old covenantal-prophetic tradition. Behind this triad of terms in Matt 23:23 are the recurring Hebrew terms of the Old Testament, *mišpaṭ, raḥam, and emeth*. When we consider this triad in the Old Testament, we can see that these terms articulate a familiar trope of faithful living. They are placed in the mouth of God when God renews and restores the Sinai covenant after the episode of the golden calf:

> The LORD, the LORD,
> a God *merciful and gracious,*
> slow to anger,
> and abounding in *steadfast love and faithfulness,*
> keeping *steadfast love* for the thousandth generation . . .
> (Exod 34:6–7)

This particular formulation is reiterated frequently in the Old Testament tradition with variations and differences of accent; see for example Num 14:18; Pss 86:15; 103:8; Jonah 4:2, and the fine review of the material by Nathan C. Lane, *The Compassionate but Punishing God: A Canonical Analysis of Exodus 34:6–7*. The terms are reiterated in the extended lamentation of Israel amid the destruction of Jerusalem and the exile:

> The *steadfast love* of the LORD never ceases,
>   his *mercies* never come to an end;
> they are new every morning;
>   great is your *faithfulness.* (Lam 3:22–23)

Indeed, these verses are nearly the only hope-filled utterance in the book of Lamentations. The same terms, moreover, are fleshed out more fully in the drama of Hosea 2 wherein God undertakes redress in order to reengage (remarry!) fickle Israel. Now the formula includes five terms:

> And I will take you for my wife forever; I will take you for my wife in *righteousness* and in *justice,* in *steadfast love,* and in *mercy.* I will take you for my wife in *faithfulness;* and you shall know the LORD.
> (Hos 2:19–20)

These five terms—that resonate with and complement the declaration of Exod 34:6–7 and the affirmation of Lam 3:22–23—constitute the sum and structure of Israel's covenantal faith, and the intent of YHWH toward Israel and toward all creation. The terms may be voiced in various patterns; but the substance is unwavering. These five terms as the main claims of faith have to do with covenantal solidarity with covenant partners in the interest and service of a viable life of reliable interaction. The entire legacy of covenantal faith in ancient Israel is fully caught and voiced in the triad of Jesus in his "woe oracle." This triad of affection, commitment, and solidarity is immensely demanding. It means giving over one's life for the sake of the other. That is what the God of Sinai has done. "You shall be for me a priestly kingdom and a holy nation" (Exod 19:6).

It could not have been foreseen at Sinai that this deep commitment would eventually entail the costliness of the embrace of Hosea 2, but that is the nature of the case. And now Jesus is calling his own contemporaries to that same practice of costly solidarity that is not only inconvenient but risky. In the horizon of Israel's covenant (that Jesus rearticulates), that is the reality of being human. To be human means to practice costly committed solidarity with others who belong to the creaturely network.

But because such covenantal existence is inconvenient and costly, the tradition is filled with attempts at lesser investment. Thus, the priestly tradition in ancient Israel settled for a codification of rules for purity and cleanliness that were less demanding than covenantal solidarity. The utterance of Jesus suggests that his contemporaries, in like manner, had found lesser ways to practice faith by an acute focus on the exactitudes of offerings. (His example is perhaps like using a calculator to figure out exactly what "tip" is required or what social gesture is expected, rather than an act of exuberant of self-giving.) The citation of "gnat and camel" in v. 24 is a glaring contrast between the *big matters of faithful humanness* and the *miniatures of spiritual commerce*. As the old priestly tradition of Israel and the parsimonious contemporaries of Jesus displaced the big claims of faith with minor matters, so now, ala Zakaria, our technological capacity draws energy and appreciation away from the claims of our humanness that depend upon serious investment for sustenance. In their place have come all-consuming "minor" preoccupations. Covenantal living means to be "all in" for the neighbor and for the common good. But once that "all in" has been traded for calculated management, the claims for the human—bravery, loyalty, generosity, faith, love—all shrivel into a society of parsimony, fear, and tribal meanness. The "majors" have been neglected; the "minors" take their place.

Not surprisingly, Karl Barth, in his great exposition of Jesus' humanity, goes further by insisting that to be human is to have a vocation, that is, a call beyond one's self: "In the light of the universalistic passages of the Bible, we can say that man in every time and place stands already in the light of life . . . It simply affirms that no one exists who is not confronted by his vocation."[4] Barth goes on to delineate the elemental human vocation in two ways. First, the bottom-line human vocation is "fellowship," that is, a common shared communal life.[5] Second, the task of human vocation is to witness to the God who gives life.[6] In Barth's extended exposition he finally arrives at the great articulation of our elemental human vocation: "As such he stands under the command to love God and his neighbor, in which there is no question of self-love, even the highest and finest."[7] The purpose of human life, a life of *vocation, fellowship, and witness* is to attest the truth of God's solidarity with us, that is, in *justice, righteousness, compassion, steadfast love, and faithfulness.*

This clear and uncompromising truth is urgent among us now as we, as in every generation, find it possible to fritter away [!] that truth to lesser matters of "mint, dill, and cumin." Technology may be at best a distraction and distortion from the main tasks of a well lived life, as the neighbor disappears from our horizon. Or at worst (with Ellul), it may constitute a threat and seduction that causes us to forget what it means to be human in a neighborly way.

Thus, we might reflect on two zones where we readily confuse the major claims with lesser, more convenient matters. First, we might reflect on the presentation of the "human" in TV commercials. It is no doubt a great gift of technology to provide ease for our life in so many ways. If, however, all we had to judge our human life were TV ads, we might readily conclude that the goal of human life is youthfulness, beauty, health, comfort, and easy longevity. Indeed, we are daily offered a panoply of drugs, most of which carry ominous threats of side effects. They promise easy and cost-free well-being. This uninterrupted focus on self-care indicates that the claims of faith cannot be easily commercialized or made marketable, so the market must invent other products for offer. The force of TV ads, unless qualified, might be read as our current example of "mint, dill, and cumin," as though they really mattered, to the neglect of weightier matters for our common life.

Second, it is a temptation in the church across the ideological spectrum to neglect the weighty gospel claims and to settle for the "mint, dill, and cumin" of easier disciplines. Indeed, it might be an urgent wake-up call

---

4. Barth, *Church Dogmatics* IV/3 second half, 491.
5. Barth, *Church Dogmatics* IV/3 second half, 539.
6. Barth, *Church Dogmatics* IV/3 second half, 575.
7. Barth, *Church Dogmatics* IV/3 second half, 593.

to the church to reflect, in some sustained specificity, on the "big five" of Hosea 2, and what that might be indicated by them for the specific practice of the church. It is astonishing how even the church community can blink away to lesser matters in order to maintain privilege or advantage or simply the status quo.

It is certain that our technological advances that Zakaria has so well noticed will not keep the church centered on its main claims. That can and will happen only when there is sustained critical study, when there is honest speech, when there are voices from "the outside," and when there is recognition that the church has a singular peculiar stake in what it is that makes us human. Zakaria's shrewd notice of "things human" is helpful. But it remains on the surface. We in the church know better than that. We know that self-giving relationships with all of the neighbors constitute the critical truth of covenantal existence. No amount of technology or product or knowledge can displace the reliability of the neighbor that is definitional for us. The great themes of relationality—*justice, righteousness, compassion, steadfast love, faithfulness*—have arisen because the sovereign Lord of creation has bound himself/herself to us for every season. From that we are also bound to each other for every season . . . all of us. No amount of mint, dill, or cumin can substitute for that self-giving binding that is the good truth of our life. It is to that binding that we are called.

8

O Land, Land, Land
(Jeremiah 22:29)
I.

The land, when it is honored and respected,
                          weeps.
It weeps long sadness
    because it knows such durable abuse.
It weeps the pollution that fouls the soil
    and stenches the sea.
It weeps for fossil heat that melts its ice.
It weeps for agribusiness that disregards natural yield.
It weeps the violence of armies to and fro in rapacious violence.
    It saddens for the anthropocene that imagines mastery rather than partnership;
    It cries all night and sheds day-time tears for the terror that begins again at sunrise.
It dares to make such lamenting noises,
    because it knows that its voice is proper and
                       legitimate and
                       God-given
    and merits being heard and heeded.
This groaning land does not know how late it is,
    nor do we.
It knows, nonetheless, that it late, very late, maybe too late.

For that reason partly protest, partly grief alongside part rage.
The tired land picks up the cadence of Jeremiah
    who witnessed royal indifference,
    elite exploitation, and
    foolishness among the chosen who assumed a blank check from the creator.
The land heard the word of the Lord,
    a word that declared the end of chosenness,
        a termination of privilege, and
        a finish to security and blessing . . .
because the creator of the earth (aka the creator of heaven)
    will not be mocked.
The earth in its sad helplessness wept the bitter tears of abandonment.

II.

The land, when dishonored and disrespected, could not weep. It had been reduced to
    inanimate object and
    insensate commodity.
It could not weep.
    It remained mute, stilled by imposition;
    it settled for numb and dumb, succumbing in obedient silence;
    it yielded passively to its uncaring masters.
The land uttered not a peep at the humiliation,
    but produced its welcome goodness for the exploiter.
The land uttered not a syllable at the threat of fossil pollution.
The soil had no heard response to the land-rape of war,
    or spoken anguish from the punishing burden of exclusion.
That mute submissive silence was just fine with Prometheus.
That possessor of fire and all things magical did not care, and
            did not listen, and
            did not notice.
The gods of endless know-how proceeded in their unthinking indifference.
    They had resources and missed signs of limit.
    The had abundant technique and missed imagination;
    They had ample explanatory theory and missed mystery.
And the land submitted, having no choice,

completely supine at the imposed vocation of production.

III.

Weeping lingers for the night,
    a long night,
        the nightmare of Descartes, Bacon, and their contemporaries,
        a long night of those who have never read Descartes or Bacon,
            but who learned their lessons deeply.
The weeping lingers for four hundred years of technology with all is
    blessings,
                    five hundred years of brutalizing slavery,
                    long centuries of modern illusion cast as reason.
But the dawn comes;
the poet anticipates: "Joy comes in the morning."
We are still pre-dawn
        pre-joy.
Nevertheless we sense a new awed knowing,
        a new alertness,
           being woke afresh...
                that land is not commodity but partner,
                that soil is not insensate but alive in praise and awe,
                that the chance for life is God-given and not self-secured.
Our moment is a time for honoring the soil,
        for respecting the land,
        for deferring to earth.
Land will speak when we listen;
It will make promises and keep them;
It will give good gifts, but in ways of its own choosing.
Land knows it is called "good," "very good," good indeed!
And then joy comes, perhaps a bit late, after dawn,
      joy for land,
      joy for all those meek who inherit the land,
      joy for all those poor and indebted who depend on the land,
           and yes, joy for the creator of the land.

9

Our Little Systems!

It is likely that most readers would not have known (or would not remember) the hymn, "Strong Son of God, Immortal Love." The first stanza goes like this:

> Strong Son of God, Immortal Love,
> Whom we, that have not seen thy face,
> By faith, and faith alone, embrace,
> Believing where we cannot prove.[1]

The words of the hymn are a poem by Tennyson titled "In Memoriam A. H. H. Obiit MDCCCXXXIII." In my growing-up church we sang this hymn often. Unfortunately, it has been dropped from many recent hymnals.

From as early as I can remember, I have loved the fifth stanza. I cannot remember a time when I did not know and sing it and love it, and I continue to sing it often:

> Our little systems have their day;
> They have their day and cease to be:
> They are but broken lights of thee,
> And thou, O Lord, art more than they.

This particular wording has summoned me yet again as I have thought about the insurrection of January 6 and the inauguration of January 20. What follows here is a reflection on that fifth stanza in light of these days of deep emergency.

---

1. Tennyson (lyrics) and Elvey (music), "Strong Son of God, Immortal Love."

Our little systems have their day. "Systems" is a quite peculiar word for a poet; it is likely Tennyson's only use of it. When we consider "system," we might think of,

- interested arrangements of *power* via nation-states;
- interested arrangements of *money* as in regressive tax laws, rigged mortgage arrangements, or the macrosystems of capitalism, communism, or socialism;
- interested arrangements of *knowledge* as in various taxonomies or even syllabii by which we teachers make a subject seem orderly; or
- interested arrangements of *belief* as in creeds and doctrines.

Tennyson's use of the term "systems," is a recognition that our conventional arrangements of power, money, knowledge, or belief do flourish, as is evident among us. They do have their day! But surely the word "system" is also recognition that these several "normal" arrangements are indeed human contrivances that are designed to flesh out *conviction* but are more elementally designed to serve particular *interests*.

We may also recognize that the term "system" might pertain to the constructed self. We are always in the process of constructing our self (selves!), both for public presentation and for self-understanding. Such constructions are characteristically tainted (as with Winnicott) by "false self." Or with the recognition that each of us is indeed "many selves" that make appearances in different venues.[2] We are able to manage such presentation of such constructed self . . . until circumstance arises that calls it all into question.

Our work of system-making in all of these different spheres is never finished. Thus the self is under construction. Thus, we rely on the regular force of liturgy to continue to construct (via interpretation) our system of knowledge and belief. And so we rely on active ideological testimony to keep our arrangements of power and money credible, even when those systems manifestly violate the facts on the ground. In his wisdom Tennyson observed that this all works . . . for a while.

They have their day and cease to be. Tennyson's poem is "In Memoriam," that is, an embrace of the reality of death. His second line in our stanza is an acknowledgement that our most treasured arrangements of self and of world have a limited shelf life and come to an end. This recognition

---

2. Schafer, *Retelling a Life*.

seems to be particularly pertinent just now as we are witnesses to an ending of some of our favorite systems, an ending that we mostly do not accept gracefully.

- We are watching the ending of patriarchy and the system of male privilege. That ending has been under way for a long while; it is not, however, completed yet.
- We are watching the ending of the system of white privilege that has marked Western culture forever. Obviously it has not ended yet, as we witness the desperate throes of white supremacy, or as we watch the assertion of the "Black Lives Matter" movement that remains highly and violently contested.
- We are witnessing the dethroning of US hegemony in international affairs with the rise of China, and with it the receding of the old claim of American "exceptionalism" that has cast the United States as God's chosen people.
- We are watching the end of a system of heterosexual moral exclusivism as we notice that gender identity is an enigmatic combination of said construction and biological givenness.
- We may be watching (we do not yet know!) the end of US democracy, as the rise of hate-filled, angry, fearful fervor is on the move with force and energy. For now the old assumptions of democracy have held, because brave, honest people have stepped up. We do not know, however, how long that courage and resolve can be sustained, or how determined is the counter resolve to an anti-democratic self-destructiveness.

It follows that when the systems of male privilege, white supremacy, national preeminence, claims of exceptionalism, and gender advantage face jeopardy, those of us who have thrived on such systemic arrangements are left more than a little displaced. That displacement generates not only eager longing for what was (nostalgia!), but also anger toward those who seem to have caused the ending of them. Thus Tennyson's second line ends an uncompromising thud: "Cease to be!" Cease to be beyond recall or recovery, gone and terminated. The poem recognizes that compelling reality of the historical process.

They are but broken lights of thee. Now for the first time the verse addresses God. We did not know it, but we are in the midst of a prayer that requires honesty and humility from us. Now our most treasured systems are no longer autonomous realities of value and wellbeing. Now they are situated in the presence of God who has until now not been mentioned. We had readily taken our systems (of whatever kind) as the real thing. We had thought that male domination was the real thing because it matched the male God of our conventional rhetoric. We had thought white supremacy was the real thing, because our best thinkers in the Enlightenment (with their inexhaustible racist taxonomies) had made the case for that, even as far as Kant! Living in an echo chamber of our own kind, it was easy enough to take our definitions of normative as settled and objective. We had thought that the United States was the last best thing, because in our oceanic isolation we had no real competitors for domination and for our version of freedom.

All of these precious arrangements seemed to be the real thing as long as we took them on their own. But now, in this third line, all of these "systems" are placed in the presence of the holiness of God. And in that presence, it is clear enough to see that they are not and could not be the real thing. They are at best "broken lights," that is, they are feeble reflectors, cracked mirrors that could never truly reflect the reality of God's will and governance. Thus this third line sets up a mighty contest between *"thee"* *(God)* and all *our little systems* that gives us skewed images of reality. We are now able to see that the modifier "little" is quite loaded and poignant. In the presence of the holy God, patriarchy is a "little" claim. In the presence of the creator of all humankind, white supremacy rings most hollow. In the presence of the Lord of all the nations, national exceptionalism is a little thing. In the presence of the God who has a preferential option for the poor, exceptionalism is an unconvincing idolatry. And so on, into our personal lives; our little posturing is set in the presence of the "image of God," the God of justice and righteousness and compassion. This third line invites us, in the presence of God, to deconstruct and abandon our "little systems" that do not adequately reflect the beaming glory of God.

And thou, O Lord, art more than they. Now the "thee" of line three is named, "Lord." The term, in the context of faith, gathers to it all the claims for God as Lord of creation, as emancipator of slaves, as restorer of exiles, as companion of the abandoned, as the bearer of life beyond our best sexuality, as rescuer of the lost, as the final Lord of Easter:

> who forgives all your iniquity,
> who heals all your diseases,

who redeems your life from the Pit,
who crowns you with steadfast love and mercy,
who satisfies you with good as long as you live. (Ps 103:3–5)

The doxologies of Israel stagger under the requirement of adequate articulation.

More than they! The "Lord" is more than the best male character. The "Lord" is more than the best white supremist. The Lord is more than the best embodiment of exceptionalism. The Lord is way more than the best case of sexuality. The Lord is more than our best selves so carefully constructed. This "more than" recalled for me the testimony of Alan Paton to his son at confirmation:

> Do not think He is a greater potentate, a manner of President of the United Galaxies,
>
> Do not think that because you know so few human beings, that He is in a comparable though more favorable position.
>
> Do not think it absurd that He should know every sparrow, or the number of hairs of your head,
>
> Do not compare Him with yourself, nor suppose your human love to be an example to shame Him.
>
> He is not greater than Plato or Lincoln, nor superior to Shakespeare or Beethoven.
>
> He is their God, their powers and their gifts proceed from him.[3]

This God outruns all of our systems and must, of necessity, stand over against them when they are filled with hubris and imagined as absolute.

This fifth stanza of the poem seems to me exactly pertinent for our moment in history. The lines of the poem invite us

- to identify our systems;
- to recognize how "little" our systems are;
- to realize that they must "cease to be";
- to see that they are, at best, cracked mirrors; and
- to recognize the overriding "Thou" who is more than any of them.

These lines can draw us very close to the crisis we now face. For a long time we have thought, in US society, that we could construct systems of realty

---

3. Paton, "Meditation for a Young Boy Confirmed."

that were beyond critique and immune to threat. And now we know better. Knowing better is an opportunity for thinking and acting otherwise. It is also an invitation to reflect (reflect upon!) the One who is more than any of our systems of management and control. Among conservatives this "more than" has been fossilized and relegated to past action. But now we know! Among progressives this "more than" has been made anemic and close to irrelevant. But now we know! Our little systems are ceasing to be before our very eyes, because this living, acting "more than they" is making all things new, new in ways that do not conform to our "little systems."

10

Providential Tyranny

"Providence" is the claim that all creation "proceeds under the fatherly care of God the creator."[1] Barth of course uses the patriarchal language of his time; he might even better have written, "the motherly care of God the creator." Providence is the affirmation that God's governance is not primarily exhibited in spectacular dramatic acts (miracles, "mighty acts"), but in the slow steady maintenance of the well-being of the world. Such governance is, perforce, hidden and does not call attention to itself; it is nonetheless the *sine qua non* for a viable life in the world. The hiddenness of God's rule does not admit to the direct exhibit of the agency of God but affirms that God's agency is nonetheless operative. Thus, for example, we can see in the great doxology of Job that there are hints of God's agency, but the matter is in reticence left largely unexpressed:

> Who has cut a channel for the torrents of rain,
>   and a way for the thunderbolt,
> to bring rain on a land where one lives,
>   on the desert, which is empty of human life,
> to satisfy the waste and desolate land,
>   and to make the ground put forth grass?
> Has the rain a father,
>   or who has begotten the drops of dew?
> From whose womb did the ice come forth,
>   and who has given birth to the hoarfrost of heaven?
> The waters become hard like stone,
>   and the face of the deep is frozen. (Job 38:25–30)

---

1. Barth, *Church Dogmatics* III/3, 3.

This hiddenness is something of a relief for those believers who are scandalized or embarrassed by the direct agency of God, and who do not want too readily to credit God with active verbs.

In his masterful exposition of the theme of "providence," Barth appeals first of all to the narrative of Genesis 22, the near sacrifice of Isaac in which it is affirmed:

> And Abraham looked up and saw a ram, caught in a thicket by his horns. Abraham went and took the ram and offered it up as a burnt offering instead of his son. So Abraham called that place, "The LORD will provide," as it is said to this day. "On the mount of the Lord it shall be provided." (v. 14)

The term we render "provide" is in Hebrew "see" (*ra'ah*):

> The word "providence" requires clarification. It is derived—and this derivation is materially important—from Genesis 2:14—the passage in which Abraham called the spot where he had been prevented from offering up Isaac, and where God's path and man's had so unexpectedly crossed . . . In this passage "to see" really means "to see about." It is an active and selective predetermining, preparing and procuring of a lamb to be offered instead of Isaac. God "sees to" this burnt offering for Abraham . . . The Lord is never absent, passive, non-responsible, or impotent, but always present, active, responsible, and omnipotent. He is never dead, but always living; never sleeping, but always awake; never uninterested, but always concerned, never merely waiting in any respect, but even where He seems to wait, even where He permits, always holding the initiative. In this consists His co-existence with the creature.[2]

God makes "provision" (*pro-video* = see before) for our creaturely needs, seeing ahead of time what is required for our well-being. It is from pro-*video* that we get "provide, provision, and providence." Thus the catechism:

> How does God constantly prove himself to be the Creator?
>
> God constantly proves himself to be the Creator by his fatherly *providence*, whereby he preserves and governs all things.
>
> What has God done for you?
>
> I believe that God has made me and all creatures; that he has given me and still preserves my body and soul, eyes, ears, and all my

---

2. Barth, *Church Dogmatics* III/3, 3, 13.

members, my reason and all my senses, also food and clothing, home and family, and all my possessions.

What does God still do for you?

God daily and abundantly *provides* me with all the necessaries of life, protects and preserves me from all danger.

Why does God do this for you?

God does all of this out of sheer fatherly and divine goodness and mercy, without any merit or worthiness on my part.³

(Yet again we have patriarchal rhetoric. It is obvious that maternal expressions would better serve the content of these affirmations.) The scripture cited by the catechism in support of these affirmations include these verses:

> He will not let your foot be moved,
>   he who keeps you will not slumber.
> He who keeps Israel
>   will neither slumber nor sleep. (Ps 121:3–4).

> The eyes of all look to you,
>   and you give them their food in due season.
> You open your hand,
>   satisfying the desire of every living thing. (Ps 145:15–16)

"Providence" is the claim that God governs the world to make it a venue for safe, secure well-being for all creatures. This innocent trust in God's goodness is given wondrous voice in the hymn, "God Will Take Care of You":

> Be not dismayed whate'er betide, God will take care of you;
> Beneath his wings of love abide, God will take care of you.
> God will take care of you, through every day, o'er all the way;
> he will take care of you, God will take care of you . . .
> All you may need he will provide, God will take care of you;
> nothing you ask will be denied, God will take care of you . . .
> No matter what may be the test, God will take care of you;
> lean, weary one, upon his breast, God will take care of you.⁴

I have been thinking about "providence" as I have been reading about "meritocracy," the notion of a society governed by those who have exceptional ability and have arrived at their power, wealth, and influence solely by the merit of their ability. Building on the work of Michael Young, *The*

---

3. *Evangelical Catechism*, 19–20.
4. Martin, "God Will Take Care of You."

Rise of Meritocracy, Michael Sandel, *The Tyranny of Merit: What's Become of the Common Good?*, has traced the way in which the notion of "merit" has eventuated in social arrangements exploitative of those who have lacked power, wealth, and access. Sandel nicely sketches the connection between the theological notion of *giftedness* and the secular notion of *success* that depends on being gifted with certain characteristics. All of such success is an outcome of God's generosity. But already with the Puritans (who performed a mediating function), the notion of a free gift of grace began to be modified into a dialectic of *grace and merit*, a dialectic notion of *helplessness and self-help*. In the end,

> The ethic of mastery and self-making overwhelmed the ethic of gratitude and humility . . . Gradually and haltingly but unmistakably, the Protestant belief in Providence . . . became a way of providing spiritual sanctions for the economic status quo . . . Providence implicitly underwrote inequalities of wealth.[5]

It turns out, in such reasoning, that the results of "merit"—wealth and power—are not only signs of grace, but they are deserved and earned:

> These days, we view success the way the Puritans viewed salvation—not as a matter of luck or grace, but as something we earn through our own effort and striving. This is at the heart of the meritocratic ethic. It celebrates freedom—the ability to control my destiny by dint of hard work—and deservingness.[6]

Having such advantaged wealth and power long enough, one can readily imagine that it is deserved. Sandel offers a compelling riff on the way in which "deserved" has entered our political vocabulary in order to assure those who "have" "deserve" what they have in disproportion; beyond that assurance it is also the recognition that there are the "deserving poor" who "merit" support. The unspoken but quite real counterpoint of this vocabulary is that there are indeed "undeserving poor" who do not help themselves and who therefore are not "entitled" to any social support. And of course, it is those with "merit" who have the ability to sort out "the deserving poor" and the "undeserving poor," a sorting out that most often has distinct racist and ethnic overtones. The notion of "deserving," moreover, has reached into consumer advertising in order to affirm that we consumers "deserve" a special product of ease or luxury.

---

5. Sandel, *Tyranny of Merit*, 41, 43.
6. Sandel, *Tyranny of Merit*, 59.

This mode of reasoning goes further to identify the "deserving poor" who have ended where they are "through no fault of their own." They are not to be blamed for their status, and so "deserve" some help. It is amazing that a political appeal on behalf of those "who through no fault of their own" most often turns out to be a particular targeted segment of the electorate. It is, moreover, curious that the verdict of "through no fault of their own" does not lead to any critical reflection on where the fault may lie if not with "them," that is, with a predatory economic system that exploits those who lack "merit."

Three outcomes arise from this self-serving, self-congratulatory reasoning. First, such reasoning leads to *hubris* among those who imagine they "deserve" extras (three scoops of ice cream!) since they have "earned it" and "it is mine." Such hubris has enormous political implications, for those with "merit" have disproportionate political clout and are "entitled" in a special way that leads not only to economic advantage but to political access, and eventually to huge tax breaks. "Merit" turned to hubris is shameless in its drive for "more" at the expense of the neighbor.

Second, the counterpoint of such shameless arrogance is to assure *humiliation* among those who lack such "merit." Whenever possible the ones with "merit" do what they can to blame the victim, to let the "left out" and "left behind" blame themselves for their sorry state. That in turn evokes deep resentment against the "merited" who ostentatiously imagine their success yields entitlement.

Third, such a contest between *hubris and humiliation* leads to the erosion of the common good, to a fear that the "undeserving" might get something for nothing, and to a kind of greedy selfishness of entitlement that only leaves more people behind, and breeds social conflict. Thus Sandel judges, "The meritocratic faith does not deliver the self-mastery it promises. Nor does it provide a basis for solidarity. Ungenerous to the losers and oppressive to the winners, merit becomes a tyrant."[7] While this is an over-simplification, it is easy to see how meritocracy has generated the kind of resentment upon which Donald Trump feeds, and which eventuates in social violence. Such a system of "merit" inevitably yields cynical conclusions: "This triumphalist aspect of meritocracy is a kind of providentialism without God, as least without a God who intervenes in human affairs . . .

---

7. Sandel, *Tyranny of Merit*, 194.

Providential Tyranny

The arc of the moral universe may bend toward justice, but God helps those who help themselves."[8]

I suggest that one biblical text that pertains directly to this drama of merit is the parable of Luke 12:13–21. The question posed at the outset of the text concerns the issue of who is entitled to financial resources (inheritance). Jesus refuses to be a probate judge to adjudicate a family dispute. Rather, he segues from a question of *financial resources* to a reflection on *covenantal reality*. His first terse response to the question promptly sets the key words out in front:

> Take care! Be on your guard against all kinds of greed; for one's life does not consist in the abundance of possessions. (Luke 12:15)

He offers three terms that the brother who posed the question had not entertained: Greed, abundance, possessions.

The parable that follows factors out these three terms. Abruptly, there is a rich man! He was a rich man engaged in agriculture. He was a prosperous knowledgeable farmer. He had *land* that produced "abundantly."

> We plow the fields and scatter the good seed on the land,
> but it is fed and watered by God's almighty hand;
> he sends the snow in winter, the warmth to swell the grain,
> the breezes and the sunshine, and soft refreshing rain.
> All good gifts around us are sent from heaven above,
> Then thank the Lord, O thank the Lord for all his love.[9]

The farmer relished his abundance. He wanted to keep it all, to store it up. He savored every grain of wheat from his productive property. He was able, moreover, to imagine that such lavish produce was his own doing.

But finally, he pauses to reflect. He said to himself! He had no one else to talk to. His abundance had isolated him. No doubt his expansive real estate meant there were no near neighbors . . . no neighborhood (see Isa 5:8–10). He hosted a party all for himself, isolated in his greedy wealth. He was not, however, alone as he imagined he was. Amid his greedy aloneness, the voice of holy reality crowded in on him. That voice "from elsewhere," first of all, calls him by his right name: "Fool." He thought himself smart, even wise. He no doubt kept up with the best agricultural journals. He was surely smart . . .but a fool. He was a fool because he failed to reckon with the given realities of his life. He failed to recognize that the land was

---

8. Sandel, *Tyranny of Merit*, 42, 58.
9. Claudius, "We Plow the Fields and Scatter."

itself a gift that kept on giving because it was God's creation sustained with rain and sunshine. He failed to recognize that abundance is a communal asset, not a private possession. He failed to consider what it cost to be "rich in things and poor in soul." He failed to acknowledge his own penultimate status was as a creature along with other creatures gifted by the creator. And because of his failure, his relished greed was a tool for his own self-destruction. He thought he "merited" all that he had; but his wealth was misdirected... not "toward God!" (v. 21), not toward his creator who "gives them their food in due season," and not toward neighbors who require food and drink. He misconstrued his place in the providence of God, and so he had deformed *God's providence* into *merit*. He likely was committed to neo-liberal economics and resented the undeserving "brothers" who wanted access to his surplus.

Not for nothing does Luke follow this story with Jesus' instruction concerning anxiety, food, clothing, and life (Luke 12:22–31). In this paragraph the raven has no "storehouse or barns," so unlike the man who needed "bigger barns"! (v. 24).[10] The *parable* (Luke 12:13–21) and the *instruction* (Luke 12:22–31) together summon to an alternative life, summon especially those of us laden with "merit" to an alternative life that is beyond the destructive interaction of hubris and humiliation.

The pastors, teachers, and interpreters in the church face our common life that now very much consists in a violent and vigorous interaction of *hubris and humiliation*. Indeed, it is plausible that many of the pastors, teachers, and interpreters in the church (myself surely included) are among those who have fostered their lives through "merit." The task of such persons, I suggest, is not to spend much energy warning church folk about such greed, for mostly greed does not pertain to church folk on a very large scale. Thus, the task is not an exercise in "morality." Rather, I suggest that this narrative of "meriting" and its loathsome outcome, in our teachable moment, is an opportunity to teach the faithful to see more clearly the *force of merit*, to see more acutely the *hubris* that largely drives public policy that assigns wealth and leverage to the "merited," to see without blinking that it is exactly such "merit" that has fueled the *resentment* and evoked the *violence* that now occupy our body politic. The interpretive task is to call attention to the ways in which our "Puritan" legacy of "work hard, get ahead, save" nurtures folk who can secure themselves and imagine they are self-made and self-sufficient.

---

10. On storehouses for surplus grain, see Exod 1:11.

Along with such discerning social analysis, the church has available its conviction about God's providential care that gives good *gifts* that refuse to be transposed into *property or possession*. They remain gifts, and gifts are for sharing. The correction to our skewed social landscape is the awareness that we all live by God's grace; the wealthy few are not self-made but depend upon an infrastructure of good gifts that are given and not earned. This general providence is affirmed in the words of Jesus:

> For he makes the sun to rise on the evil and on the good,
> and sends rain on the righteous and on the unrighteous.
> (Matt 5:45)

Our social reality, however, has skewed that grace-filled reality:

> It rains on the just and on the unjust fella,
> but the rain hits the just fella
> because the unjust has taken his umbrella.

The neighborhood is in the umbrella business. It is, moreover, neighborly work to assure that all the neighbors receive and benefit from God's good gifts.

11

Psalm 29

FIRST SUNDAY AFTER EPIPHANY; THE BAPTISM OF CHRIST

It is the hunch of some scholars (including me) that Psalm 29 is a liturgical script (or an echo of a liturgical script) that served an annual pageant in the Jerusalem temple in ancient Israel. The intent of that pageant was to perform a drama whereby YHWH was designated as King of the gods for the coming year. The pageant featured a contest among the gods to see who best qualified for that designation; but of course the outcome was assured (rigged?) for YHWH by the shape of the drama. I invite you, dear reader, to entertain (for now) that scholarly hunch in order to see how it may illumine our reading of the Psalm:

The Psalm readily divides into four *unequal* parts:

1. In vv. 1–2, YHWH is promoted as a candidate for God for the coming year and is commended by the singers of the Psalm. They bid for praise for YHWH with the opening imperatives. Notice that the name, YHWH, is reiterated four times, not unlike a political nominating speech in which the candidate's name is mentioned as often as possible. The imperative "ascribe" is addressed to "the sons of gods," so that the poetry imagines a liturgic contest being conducted in heaven among the gods, as if the gods were to choose a "chief god" for the next year. Notice the double use of "glory" to which we will return.

2. In vv. 3–9a, the main body of the Psalm, like every other candidate YHWH must perform a feat of power in order to show why and in what way YHWH is eligible to become God for the coming year. It is often noted that the term "voice" occurs seven times, a perfect number to characterize a perfect action. These verses in fact portray a mighty storm; YHWH is portrayed as a storm God, appropriating some of the action and force of the old Canaanite storm God, Baal. The purpose of these verses is to underscore the massive power of YHWH who is thereby commended as the real God. The geography of these verses trace a mighty rainstorm that breaks over the Mediterranean Sea, hits the cedar trees on the coast of Lebanon, and sweeps down into the wilderness of Kadesh to the south; it is all taken as an exhibit of uncommon divine power. This is the God who can ride on the rain clouds, bring the waters, and cause ruin in the wake of the storm (see Deut 33:26; Pss 68:4; 104:3; and Nah 1:3). We can imagine, within the confines of the drama, that the other gods perform their great feats; none of them can rival the power of YHWH.

3. At the end of this mighty performance, in v. 9b, all those who have witnessed this mighty performance are invited to "vote," to indicate their preference for the "head god" for the coming year. The vote is unanimous! "All cry 'glory.'" *All* assert that YHWH is best qualified to be the king-god. *All* are mightily impressed with the power of YHWH. *All* conclude that no other god can compete with YHWH. Within the liturgy, the "all" would include "the sons of God'" in heaven and all the faithful gathered in the temple. It would also include all the other creatures who gather in awe before their creator, all fire and hail, all snow and frost, stormy wind, mountains, hills, fruit trees, cedars, wild animals, cattle, creeping things, flying birds, kings and princes (see Ps 148:7–11). *All* in heaven and earth are agreed: YHWH is God; to him sound glory. Or as we familiarly pray, "Thine is the kingdom, the power, and the glory."

4. Finally, after the mighty performance and the assertion of "all" who witnessed the performance, YHWH is newly enthroned as king (vv. 10–11). Verse 10, in doxological language, imagines that YHWH is now conducted to the throne where sits the confirmed God-king for the coming year. But notice, the throne of God is "over the flood." In v. 3 the "mighty waters" had been a force of rebellious chaos. But now those same flood waters that surge around and threaten the earth have all been tamed and settled. Those waters are now completely in obedience to the Lord of creation, so still and settled and stable that the divine throne can be situated there. God has fully

mastered chaos (see Mark 4:35–41)! And from that newly situated throne the new Lord of all creation issues a blessing (or benediction). The blessing is for "his people." The term, twice voiced, may refer to Israel. But since this is the Lord of all creation, it may count all people as "his people." The new God-king declares a new reign of **peace** (*shalom*) that will put an end to the chaos just witnessed.

Thus, the liturgy performs the narrative of how the lived experience of chaos (in both history and "nature") is tamed and made into an obedient subject of YHWH, now destined to do the will of the creator. It may be, indeed, that this liturgy served its reassuring purpose in times of great historical upheaval, so that the liturgy performs a counter-reality, counter to what is known and lived in the life of the world.

It may be that it will strike you as odd to think that anyone in the orbit of biblical faith could, concerning such serious matters, engage in such playful imagination. If you think that, I want you to consider, in light of the foregoing, what happens in and through the liturgy in the two great inflection points of the Christian liturgical year.

Consider Christmas. Of course we know that Jesus as a historical figure was born in Bethlehem of Judea long ago. In our Christmas pageants, however, we telescope the years from then until now and intend to make that ancient birth real life present tense. Thus, we are able to sing, even when we know better:

> Give ye heed to what we say: News, news!
> Jesus Christ is born *today!*
> Ox and ass before him bow,
> and he is in the manger now.
> Christ is born today, Christ is born today![1]

> On *this day* earth shall ring
> with the song children sing to the Lord, Christ our King,
> born on earth to save us;
> him the Father gave us.
> Ideooo, ideooo, ideo gloria in excelsis Deo.[2]

Even when we do not sing "today" or "this day," we still sing present tense as if the birth were now. We sing "today" or "this day" because the liturgical

---

1. Neale, "Good Christian Friends, Rejoice."
2. Joseph, "On This Day Earth Shall Ring."

performance has a quality of reality of its own, not unlike, I suggest, the pageant of kingship for YHWH in ancient Israel.

> Joy to the world, the Lord is come!
> Let earth receive her King.
> Let every heart prepare him room,
> and heaven and nature sing.[3]

Now is the time of birth and coming. *Now* is the time for joy. *Now* is the time of the "wonder of his love."

Or consider Easter. We confess that Jesus was executed by the Roman governor and raised three days later. Nonetheless, in our singing the accent is upon "today" as the day of resurrected life:

> Christ the Lord is risen *today,* Alleluia!
> Earth and heaven in chorus sing, Alleluia!
> Raise your joys and triumphs high, Alleluia!
> Sing, ye heavens and earth rely, Alleluia![4]

In our singing we are able telescope the times and let it be "today," as the day of new life. For that glorious day we muster our best music, our best flowers, and our best preaching in order to re-perform that wonder of new life.

Thus we are able to see that both Christmas and Easter are pageants of wonder whereby the church, in its liturgical imagination, brings these ancient memories to present tense as doxological reality. It is not much of a strain, after such considerations, to think that ancient Israel, in its own doxological imaginative dialect in the Psalm, could employ the same transport of wonder concerning the rule of YHWH *from then to now, from there to here.*

When we consider the mighty performance of YHWH as certification to be qualified to be king of the gods, we can transfer that performance in the Psalm to King Jesus. We may do so when we reiterate the mighty powers of the storm God to the transformative ways of King Jesus. The mighty performance of Jesus, however, is not to wreak havoc as does that ancient storm toward the sea, cedars and the desert. Jesus' mighty work, rather, is to transform disabled creation and dysfunctional humanity that is visibly (but not exclusively) embodied among the blind, the lame, lepers, the poor, and the dead. When the church recites the mighty deeds of Jesus that exhibit his rule they are of a very different ilk from that of the ancient storm god:

3. Watts, "Joy to the World."
4. Wesley, "Christ the Lord Is Risen Today."

> The blind receive their sight, the lame walk, lepers are cleansed, the deaf hear, the dead are raised, the poor have good news brought to them. (Luke 7:22)

These specific transformations are markers of the Lordship of Jesus. This is the one who commands the demons and the powers of death. Indeed, we may imagine that every time the church gathers to sing its doxologies to Jesus, it is re-performing the liturgy whereby Jesus is made king yet again. Jesus is indeed "king of kings" and "Lord of Lords," and that reality cannot be re-performed too often. He is, as we sing, Lord of all our history. But he is, as we also sing, Lord of heaven and earth, of nature as well as history:

> Fairest Lord Jesus, ruler of all nature,
> O thou of God and man the Son,
> thee will I cherish, thee will I honor,
> thou my soul's glory, joy and crown.
> Jesus is fairer . . . Jesus is purer . . . Jesus shines purer . . .[5]

Thus on all counts we can let Psalm 29 serve, in Christian imagination, for *our Christmas*, for *our Easter*, for *our Epiphany*, for *our every worship* and *our every doxology*. All can exclaim "Glory" as did the angels over Bethlehem. And when we hear the opening glory of the Psalm, we can listen for the concluding "peace" of the Psalm, the peace sung at Bethlehem:

> **Glory** to God in the highest,
>   and on earth peace among those whom he favors (Luke 2:14).

It is no wonder that the wise men appear in Epiphany:

> Wise men from the East came to Jerusalem asking, "Where is the child who has been born king of the Jews? For we observed his star at its rising, and have come to pay him homage. (Matt 2:2)

King indeed! It is no wonder that "heaven and nature sing"!

---

5. Anonymous, "Fairest Lord Jesus."

12

Psalm 107:1–3, 17–22

FOURTH SUNDAY IN LENT

LENT IS A TIME when we ponder our "dustiness," our morality and our fragility. In the orbit of faith, Lent is a time when we think and pray most deeply about our *dependence upon God;* we recognize that we ourselves are not fully and finally able to cope with life in its extremities. For such pondering, thinking, and praying about our dependence upon God there is no better practice than the regularity and intentionality of *gratitude*. Gratitude is the active embrace of the truth that we live by God's good gifts that are generously and freely given to us. In honest gratitude we arrive at Paul's questions:

> What do you have that you did not receive? And if you have received it, why do you boast if it were not a gift? (1 Cor 4:7)

And then we reach Paul's answer to his own questions. We have nothing that is not a gift from God. Gratitude is the glad recognition that we live by good gifts.

For that reason Psalm 107 in the lectionary is a fitting text for Lent, because it is the fullest voicing that we have in scripture of gratitude that consists in (a) naming our circumstances of need, (b) identifying God's good rescue to our need with some specificity, and (c) responding in doxological affirmation to the God who hears, gives, and saves. The psalm offers four representative "cases" of human extremity (to which we may add many others (including the pandemic) concerning in turn *desert wandering* (vv. 4–9), *prison* (vv. 10–16), *sickness* (vv. 17–22), and *storm at sea* (vv. 23–32). In its characteristic parsimony the lectionary allows us only one of these four instances of need and rescue, but the wise interpreter will feel free to take up the entire Psalm and not accept that ill-advised imposed limit. A good reason for doing the entire Psalm is that the repetition of the pattern of *need, rescue, and thanks* is important for both the cadence of the Psalm itself and for our own pattern of gratitude whereby we acknowledge our glad dependence upon the goodness of God.

In order to appreciate the pattern of gratitude, we might consider in turn each of these accent points that recur in each "case" of human extremity. First, each "case" portrays a *human predicament* in which the human agent is helpless and can do nothing for rescue or wellbeing. This includes:

- A lack of food and drink in the wilderness, in the Bible a zone that runs beyond the reach of God (v. 5).
- Prison marked by darkness, gloom, and misery (v. 10).
- Sickness that draws near to death (v. 17). This lectionary episode might make a particular link to the pandemic.
- Peril in a sea storm that is described in extended graphic detail, "at their wits end" (vv. 23–27).

All of these cases bespeak human vulnerability and helplessness.

Second, in each case the appropriate and prompt response to extremity is *urgent appeal to God*: "They cried to the Lord" (vv. 6, 13, 19, 25). The human agents knew what to do as women and men of faith. They knew, in their helplessness and vulnerability, to turn to the God who cares for them. This ready turn to prayer reminds me of the exchange in the catechism of my youth:

> What does God still do for you?
>
> God daily and abundantly provides me with all necessaries of life, protects and preserves me from all danger.
>
> Why does God do this for you?
>
> God does all this out of sheer fatherly and divine goodness and mercy, without any merit or worthiness on my part.[1]

1. *Evangelical Catechism*, 20 (questions 17 and 18).

Psalm 107:1–3, 17–22

Third, in every case *God answers* promptly and effectively:

> He delivered them out of their distress;
> he led them by a straight way,
> until they reached an inhabited town. (vv. 6b–7)

> He saved them from their distress;
> he brought them out of darkness and gloom,
> and broke their bonds asunder. (vv. 13b–14)

> He saved them from their distress;
> he sent out his word and healed them,
> and delivered them from destruction. (vv. 19b–20)

> He brought them out from their distress;
> He made the storm be still,
> and the waves of the sea were hushed . . .
> He brought them to their desired haven. (vv. 28b–29, 30b)

God's response is immediate, without pause, in the same verses as the outcry. There is no space or delay between "cry out" and God's response. The responses are as prompt as that of a parent to a child who cries out in the night! (See Matt 7:7–11.)

Fourth, the effective response of God in each case is seen by the Psalmist as an *embodiment of "tenacious solidarity"* (*hesed*, that is, covenantal love).

> Let them thank the LORD for his steadfast love,
>   for his wonderful works to humankind. (v. 8)
> Let them thank the LORD for his steadfast love,
>   for his wonderful works to humankind. (v. 15).
> Let them thank the LORD for his steadfast love,
>   for his wonderful works to humankind. (v. 21)
> Let them thank the LORD for his steadfast love,
>   for his wonderful works to humankind. (v. 31)

That tenacious solidarity, moreover, in each case leads to a "wonderful work," that is, a staggeringly inexplicable act of transformation that goes beyond all of our expectations and explanations. The conventional word for such an act is "miracle," but that term does not adequately reflect the free agency of God who acts in faithful covenantal freedom.

Only after this repeated four-fold sequence do we arrive at *thanks* (vv. 8, 15, 22, 31) as the fifth element in the pattern of this Psalm. The jussive invitation to thanks is terse and uninflected. But we have two clues about how thanks is to be performed in v. 22:

> And let them offer thanksgiving sacrifices,
> and tell of his deeds with songs of joy.

First, the ones who receive the gift of life from YHWH are to tell of God's goodness with some specificity. This is what happens four times in this Psalm. Thanks is story-telling in the congregation so that others may also know and come to trust in the good transformative actions of YHWH. The point is reiterated in v. 32; and in v. 2, the redeemed who have benefitted are to "say so." Thanks is witnessing in detail to the gift of life from YHWH as in Psalm 30. Thanks is an out-loud action that tells the narrative of rescue. That is why Claus Westermann, the great Psalm scholar, has listed songs of thanks as "narrative Psalms."[2] Second, the same verse adds another action:

> Let them offer thanksgiving sacrifices. (v. 22a)

Thanks includes material acts of generosity that are given back to the God who gives all good gifts. Thank offerings are liturgically offered up to God; but practically such an offering is something of material value that is contributed to the support and wellbeing of the community. It is for that reason that in much of the contemporary church there are "thanks offerings" that are sums of money that are variously dispatched for missional actions of care and relief. By both *word* and *material gesture* the faithful articulate and exhibit their glad dependence upon the God who gives life. The witness of word is in order that others may come to share in that glad honest dependence. The material gesture is that others may benefit from the God upon whom we all depend.

Notice how both of these actions that together constitute thanks are counter to the dominant ideology of the commoditized, autonomous self. That commoditized, autonomous self is not likely to recognize any dependence upon any other. If that self is successful, it can easily imagine it is self-made. If that self is unsuccessful, our society will effectively help it feel a sense of failure and shame. Thus both the pride-filled successful self and the shame-filled unsuccessful self together are not likely to embrace glad dependence on the goodness of God. As a result neither is likely to "say so," (v. 2), "to tell of his deeds" (v. 22), or to "extol him" in the congregation (v. 32). We are reluctant to tell the story of how our lives depend upon

---

2 Westermann, *The Psalms*, 71–80.

the inexplicable goodness of God. In like manner, the commoditized, autonomous self is not likely to commit a deliberate act of material generosity. Amid an ideology of scarcity we are wont to believe that there is not enough to go around, and we had better keep what we have. And surely we do not want our hard earned materiality to go to anyone who is "undeserving," given our ideological conviction that we ourselves are "deserving" of whatever we ourselves have. Thus our dominant value system works powerfully against both our "telling" and our "offering" in ways that outlandishly match the goodness of God.

Thus when the faithful, as the speaker in this Psalm, commit these two acts of gratitude, they participate in a subversive, counter-cultural reality that attests we are not self-made, self-sufficient, or autonomous. Our lives, rather, are derived from and depend upon the goodness of the God who attends to our needs. The faithful who engage in such daring acts of gratitude as telling and giving are not simple-minded. We are fully wise to the world and know very well the powerful force of knowledge, of money, and of power. In committing gratitude, however, we embrace an act of "second naiveté," as we slide beyond all the wisdom of the world that we know and move toward the more elemental reality of our lives. That is, we come to see that all that we are and have has been received as a gift.

In light of this Psalm, the work of Lent is to move our lives more fully into the practice of gratitude expressed in telling and giving. This move entails a willful departure from the dominant ideology of our culture that takes the form of pride among the successful or that takes the form of shame among the unsuccessful. It turns out that amid the goodness of God, neither our pride nor our shame counts for anything. A life given over to the telling and the giving may become unencumbered by either pride or shame, unencumbered enough to be lost in "wonder, love, and praise." The ones who steadily practice thanks can, with the Psalmist, gladly affirm:

> He raises up the needy out of their distress,
>   and makes their families like flocks. (v. 41)

It is no wonder that the final word of this Psalm is that we may "consider the steadfast love (tenacious solidarity) of the LORD" (v. 43). We have nothing better to think about!

13

Refusing Erasure

IN MY RECENT EXPOSITION of Mary and Joseph on their way to Bethlehem ("On Becoming a Statistic") I noted that they went there to be "registered" (Luke 2:1–5). They were "written down" by the Roman Empire for purposes of taxation; we know, moreover, that the empire never forgets the name of a single taxpayer. Now in what follows here, I pursue a countertheme, namely that the empire readily *erases* the names of persons it finds "unqualified," unwelcome, or simply inconvenient for the purposes of empire. The dominant culture has many strategies for accomplishing "good riddance" that run from neglect and abandonment, to economic dismissal, to incarceration or deportation, or to even more brutal measures of disappearance and erasure. It is chilling indeed that "disappear" has become a transitive verb, so that we can say that the regime "disappeared" someone. While Mary and Joseph were written down by the empire forever, many young children were brutally "disappeared" by Herod, leaving only mother Rachel to grieve them (Matt 2:16–18).

While I was aware of this practice by brutalizing regimes, I have become more fully and acutely aware of it by reading *What You Have Heard Is True: A Memoir of Witness and Resistance* by Carolyn Forché. Forché is a U.S. poet who was invited (recruited!) by Leonel Gómez Vides to come to El Salvador to observe and learn of the political brutality of his country. Gomez was an elusive but effective activist for justice and peace, and was one of the brokers of the peace agreement in El Salvador in 1992 that put political society on a new democratic footing. Forché accepted his invitation and spent extended periods with Gomez, amid daily danger, as she experienced his society permeated with violence and with the threat of violence. She has written of her experience, one of the most important and most searing books I have read. I commend it to you.

Forché experienced the competing brutalities of the government and a number of left-wing guerilla groups who were unrestrained in their capacity to cause suffering, torture and disappearance. She also observed the pervasive fear in which people lived, how secrecy had to be practiced, and how those under threat were required to move constantly to another safe place while no one was ever fully safe. Forché writes of the "disappeared":

> All that day we went places together—to the empty gray cathedral without pews, flocks of doves flying the clerestory; to the human rights office, with its red-and-gray-tiled floor, folding chairs and blue walls, where she [Margarita] showed me photograph albums, one with daisies on the cover, where the photos of the *desaparecidos* were mounted on sticky pages covered with plastic. Most of the photographs of the *desaparecidos* had been taken at school or on some occasion, such as completion of nurses' training, a *quinceanera* birthday party, or dinner in celebration of a betrothal. Therefore, most of the photos were of young people, even if, at the time they disappeared, some were no longer young.[1]

The brutality served not only to erase those who might threaten power, but also to intimidate those who might undertake resistance. The wonder of her report is that there was a considerable sustained and courageous resistance movement, even in the face of such acute danger.

I read this book over Christmas week, a gift from my son. It happens that in my church, Central United Methodist Church, on the Sunday after Christmas we remember by name those who have died in our town in the last year because of a lack of adequate housing. (We call them "homeless," as if that classification that is partly an indictment of them explains everything.) My church, led by the indefatigable pastor Jane Lippert, maintains (along with others in our community) a vigorous ministry of care, food, and shelter for those without adequate housing. But of course even given such good attentiveness, it is "inevitable" (!) that some of those exposed to these severe Michigan winters will die. Thus on December 27, the last Sunday of the year we once again remembered in church by name thirteen such persons who died in the last year for lack of adequate housing.

---

1. Forché, *What You Have Heard*, 133.

Thirteen is not a big number. But it is a number! It is a number that measures the neglect of our community and the lack of an adequate public care system. The thirteen persons and their names will not be remembered very long. They are readily "disappeared" by a wealthy economy that lacks the political will to provide a caring humane infrastructure for all the neighbors. "Homelessness" is caused by a lack of housing. Of course I do not equate that *uncaring violence* in our town with the *cynical brutality* of El Salvador. But they are of a piece. Both rosters of the dead, those remembered in El Salvador and those remembered in Traverse City together point to a violent society in which violence becomes so commonplace as to be unnoticed.

The counter-community of the church (along with its allies) has as a part of its work the refusal of such erasure, resisting the nullification of human persons. Thus our remembering is a vigorous political activity. In my church we paused to remember, even if not in any durable way, assured that at least Pastor Jane knew these well-beloved persons.

Forché reports more daring efforts at remembering in El Salvador:

> In the human rights office, these albums and some other folders were stacked high on a table. There was a telephone, and a fan turning side to side. People came and went, mostly older women. Some appeared desperate and anxious, clutching photos and scraps of paper, while others stared listlessly, waiting for some news. I turned the plastic pages, and it was like looking through a school yearbook of those most likely never to be seen again. I wrote as many names as I could in my notebook, not knowing yet what I would do with them. No one stopped me from copying these names down. A woman even crossed the room to bring me another album from the table, nodding as she pressed it into my hands.[2]

Toward the end of her book Forché returns to the practice of remembering:

> When a body was found that matched, it would be placed in a coffin, sometimes with a window cut over the face so that the mourners could see that yes, this was indeed that brother or friend, and the coffin would be taken to the altar for Sunday Mass, where Monsenor Romero welcomed them, and recited their names into microphones, so the names would be heard throughout the basilica or the cathedral, and also on the radio and in the streets. It didn't matter how many names. He called out all of them.[3]

2. Forché, *What You Have Heard*, 133.
3. Forché, *What You Have Heard*, 365.

It strikes me that this defiant act of calling out each name was not unlike our liturgical practice at Central Church, only much more immediately dangerous. In both cases, the act was an act of resistance and defiance. In both cases it was an act to refuse erasure. In El Salvador, it was resistance and defiance of *great brutality*. In Traverse City it was resistance and defiance against *uncaring neglect*. In both cases it was an act that mattered; in both cases, however, it was an act that did not change anything. Even after such remembering, the dead are indeed disappeared.

But then I remembered one other matter. In the later biblical tradition, with the emergence of apocalyptic imagery, there was a shift from utterance to *document*, from oral practice to *written evidence*. The great apocalyptic seers were authors and sponsors of written witnesses. In the orbit of such documentary thinking (real or imagined), the biblical tradition develops the imagery of a written "Book of Life" that is secure beyond all historical vagaries. This "Book of Life" contains the mysteries and secrets that are most closely held by the holy God of heaven and earth. This includes the decisions made by the holy one concerning the shape and outcome of the future. Once that imagery is developed, moreover, appeal can be made to it after the exhaustion and failure of all penultimate assurances.

An entry point into this remarkable imagery is found in Luke 10:20. The seventy disciples return from their mission with exuberant success:

> The seventy returned with joy, saying, "Lord, in your name even the demons submit to us!" He said to them, "I watched Satan fall from heaven like a flash of lightning. See, I have given you authority to tread on snakes and scorpions, and over all the power of the enemy; and nothing will hurt you." (vv. 17–19)

Jesus confirms their great success and their joy. But then he turns their attention away from their "success" to a much more elemental affirmation:

> Nevertheless, do not rejoice at this, that the spirits submit to you, but rejoice that your names are *written in heaven*. (v. 20)

The joy of the disciples is misplaced if it is because of their "success." Rather, their joy should be found in the assurance that their names are recorded in the script of God. This rhetoric imagines a great ledger kept beyond human writing. In that record are the names of faithful who will, in all times to come and beyond all time, be remembered and cherished "in heaven." They are entered because of their faithfulness to the gospel.

We may notice other appeals to this same imagery. In the book of Daniel, there will be deliverance for the wise and the righteous:

> At that time Michael, the great prince, the protector of your people, shall arise. There shall be a time of anguish, such as has never occurred since the nations first came into existence. But at that time your people shall be delivered, everyone who is found *written in the book*. Many of those who sleep in the dust of the earth shall awake, some to everlasting life, and some to the shame and everlasting contempt. Those who are wise shall shine like the brightness of the sky, and those who lead many to righteousness, like the stars forever and ever. But you, Daniel, keep the words secret and *the book* sealed until the time of the end. (Dan 12:1–4)

"Anguish" makes reference to the hard time of Antiochus IV who assaulted the Jews for their Jewishness. In Malachi, the urgency is a bit more extended and concerns the fear of the Lord:

> Those who revered the LORD spoke with one another. The LORD took note and listened, and *a book of remembrance was written before him* of those who revered the Lord and thought of his name. They shall be mine, says the LORD of hosts, my special possession on the day when I act, and will spare them as parents spare their children who serve them. Then once more you shall see the difference between the righteous and the wicked, between the one who serves God and one who does not serve him. (Mal 3:16–18)

The prophet uses the phrase "special possession" *(sglh)*, an appeal to the older tradition for the special status of Israel (see Exod 19:5; Deut 7:6; 14:2; 26:18). Only now the term refers to those who "revered the LORD," who practiced risky righteousness, and who have been written down. The imagery is reiterated in the New Testament in the promissory vision of the book of Revelation:

> If you conquer, you will be clothed like them in white robes, and I will not blot your names out of *the book of life*; I will confess your name before my Father and before his angels. (Rev 3:5; see 13:8)

In all of these uses the ones whose names are recorded in *the Book of Life* are those who have remained faithful in demanding circumstance. In the book of Daniel the demand concerned those who were faithful under Antiochus. In the book of Malachi it is those who remained faithful amid cultural accommodation. And in the book of Revelation it is those who withstood the threats and dangers of the Roman Empire.

And, of course, we notice a word of negation toward all those who do not have their names written in the Book of Life. They, like Antiochus and the Roman rulers, might be written down in monuments, plaques, and mausoleums; they are not, however, written in the Book of Life and they will not be remembered very long at all. We may readily imagine that in El Salvador the names written in the Book of Life are those who have withstood the pressures of brutality and death and have kept a vision and practice of humanity. And even in Traverse City we may wonder about ourselves, who will be written down in the Book of Life and who will not.

The names written in *the Book of Life* are beyond the reach of our historical control. We do not write the entries into the Book. We may imagine, nonetheless, that the recitals of the names by Archbishop Oscar Romero and by Pastor Jane Lippert constitute reliable, significant human echoes of the heavenly book. The Book of Life refuses to accept the "disappearance" and the erasure caused by either brutality or neglect. Human pride and illusion can imagine who will be long remembered for their power and wealth. But such fantasy has no reliable durability. By contrast, *the Book of Life*, inscribed beyond us at the throne of good mercy, makes a different kind of record. It seems, as I write this in Traverse City, a long leap from *The Book of Life* to policy and practice in my town. But of course those whose names are written down are the ones who know how matters are reckoned. They know that readiness to combat disappearance and refusal to erase is daily work in the neighborhood. The book is being written on its next pages even as we breathe. Recitals of the names by Oscar and Jane attest an alternative to the name established by power and wealth or by cozy award systems. Shift the imagery for a final moment. The good shepherd knows the name of every sheep. Equally amazing is the claim that the sheep know the shepherd (John 10:11–18). The sheep are remembered and cherished long after the "wild beasts" have been forgotten and erased.

14

Return to Normal?

EVERYONE WANTS TO GET back to normal after Covid-19. All of us have had our lives disrupted. Well, maybe not everyone yearns for that old normal. More men than women want to return to how it was then. More white people than people of color want to return to that old normal. More straight persons than LGBTQ people want that old normal. That is, the more we have been privileged, advantaged, and empowered, the more want to go back there.

It is clear in any case that our "return to normal" cannot be simple, direct, or in a straight line. Very much has changed irreversibly and will not be restored. It remains to be seen what the new normal may be; it will in any case require careful and broad negotiation, precisely because some of the folk among us who have not been privileged, advantaged, and empowered heretofore do not want to go back, and do not intend to go back. They want to go forward to a new normal that we have not known before. It belongs to the hard work of faith to be engaged in that negotiation and in the shaping of the new normal that will be partly the old renewed and partly newness never before imagined:

> Therefore every scribe who has been trained for the kingdom of heaven is like the master of a household who brings out of his treasure *what is new* and *what is old*. (Matt 13:52)

In the Old Testament the disruptive fissure that posed in stark terms "back to normal" questions was the destruction of Jerusalem and the deportation of leading public figures into exile. Given that great disruption, it was inevitable that some would ask, "What comes next?" In the prophetic tradition of ancient Israel, I can identify two texts that reflect a wonderment and expectation about the future. There are more than two such texts, but these two texts contain a particularly distinctive phrasing.

In Isa 1:21–26, the poetry announces the primary themes of the book of Isaiah that are to come:

The failure of the city of Jerusalem (vv. 21–23);

The devastation of the city (vv. 24–25).

In v. 26 the poem begins to reflect on what comes after the devastation:

> And I will restore your judges as *at the first*,
> and your counselors as at the beginning. (v. 26a)

Two things strike me about this rhetoric. First, there is the verb "restore" (*shuv*). God will return Israel to its life. Second, this verse uses a quite distinctive term, "at first" (or "in the beginning"). The substance of this half verse is that the restoration will be to a form of social existence that reflects "your judges," that is, that reflects a small rural economy known in the book of Judges without large urban centers. Such an existence was sure to be precarious, given the ready potential for unregulated violence. On the other hand, this existence was much more immediately aware of a theological dimension to lived reality, alert to the force of God's governance. Thus in the book of Judges the rendering of social history is according to a covenantal formula of disobedience-judgment-petition-rescue (see the formula in Judg 3:7–11). While this formula is a rather heavy-handed imposition upon memory, such a memory and such a restoration will be without the pomp of the temple, without the security of a large military apparatus, without highly developed technology, and without the reach of an international economy. The governance of God was engaged much more directly. There would be no larger human governance that could impose order, provide protection, or engage in exploitation. It is a life marked by intense political vulnerability. That is the "at first" that the prophet anticipates in v. 26a.

But then, in v. 26b, prophetic expectation extends further with an abrupt "afterword." After a time of "at first" vulnerability, there will be a city.

> Afterward you shall be called the city of righteousness,
> the faithful city. (v. 26)

That anticipated city is surely Jerusalem, a city that in time to come will be marked by righteousness and faithfulness, the very characteristics that were lacking in the condemnation of v. 21! It is as though the prophet anticipates that after the disruption of the exile Israel will again enact the sequence of its ancient history *from rural to urban, from judges to kings, from vulnerability to an ordered society*. The poem does not articulate a time frame. It does not tell us how long it will be until "afterward." Thus the poem ponders the future according to the models of society rooted in old memory.

A second text that claims our attention is in Jer 3:7:

> I will restore the fortunes of Judah and the fortunes of Israel,
>   and rebuild them as they were *at first*.

As in Isa 1:26, this verse also uses the verb "restore" (*shuv*). Only here it is used three times, "restore, fortunes, fortunes." The "fortunes" are that which is restored. Moreover, the text, like Isa 1:26, uses the term "at first." These are the only two verses that use this exact same form. Thus Jeremiah, like Isaiah, is considering what will come after the great disruption. The verse uses the term "rebuild" that sounds not unlike an anticipation of "Build Back Better." In the next verse, the anticipated restoration is given a more explicitly religious tilt:

> I will cleanse them from all the guilt of their sin against me,
> and I will forgive all the guilt of their sin and rebellion against me.
> (v. 8)

The governing verbs are "cleanse," an act of purification via purgation, and "forgive." The poetry does not suggest exactly how "cleanse" and "forgive" are linked to rebuilding; clearly the poetry intends a systemic, wholesale recovery from the disruption.

When, however, we consider the entire chapter in Jeremiah 33, it is unmistakably clear that the prophet is not settled on one single scenario of restoration. Chapter 33 consists in a variety of scenarios of restoration that seem to be arranged without any overall design, that is, rather happenstance. Two of these scenarios have claimed my attention. On the one hand, vv. 12–13 offer a bucolic anticipation of an economy based on sheep. These lines expect that everywhere, in every region of the land, shepherding will prosper.

> In this place that is waste, without human beings or animals, and in all its towns there shall again be pasture for shepherds resting their flocks. In the Shephelah and of the Negeb, in the land of

Benjamin, the places around Jerusalem and in the towns of Judah, flocks shall again pass under the hand of the one who counts them, says the Lord. (vv. 12–13)

For shepherding to prosper, moreover, there must be a stable social order without threatening or rampaging armies or predatory urban power. The vulnerable shepherds featured in the anticipated economy are not unlike those later shepherds who, near Bethlehem, were, "living in the fields, keeping watch over their flocks by night" (Luke 2:8).

It is striking that through an editorial process the next scenario of hope that follows in the text, placed back-to-back with this company of shepherds, is an anticipation of the restoration of the Davidic monarchy (Jer 33:14–16; see 23:5–6). Only now, Davidic rule, unlike the sordid failure of the regime in the run-up to the Babylonian disruption (see 2 Kgs 24–25), will be marked by justice and righteousness. The imagery of a reconstituted monarchy is extended in the next promissory paragraph that assures that God's covenant with David is as sure as the covenant that orders creation (vv. 19–22; see Ps 89:3–4, 33–37). We have seen in the Isaiah text, the *rustic image of Judges* and the *urban scenario of Jerusalem* are sequenced, one after the other. In the rendering of Jeremiah, by contrast, there is no such sequencing. There are only two scenarios of restoration on offer that are placed back-to-back.

When we consider Isa 1:26 and Jer 33:7 together, we have the only two prophetic texts that speak of a return "as at first." Thus we may discern in these two texts the articulation of something of a pattern. It will be "as at first":

- Isaiah: a bucolic restoration of judges . . . afterward . . . a restored city of justice and righteousness;

- Jeremiah: a rustic reemergence of a shepherd economy . . . a restored monarchy of righteousness.

Both prophetic traditions offer a glimpse into the future that consists in more than one model of social order. Both models are rooted in memory, and the prophets do not adjudicate which of them is preferable. This twice offered double model suggests that restoration, in prophetic expectation, is not and cannot be a straight line anticipation or a straight line prediction. (We may notice that in the gospel narrative of Jesus we can see the same two models articulated if we pay attention to the geography of the narrative. Thus Jesus' ministry is in Galilee; "Galilee" functions as a narrative cipher for a less regulated society occupied by marginal people, whereas "Jerusalem" is an embodiment of wealth, power, and regulation. The preference in the gospel narrative is clearly for "Galilee.") Prophetic expectation is, rather, an open-ended hope that has confidence in God's restorative capacity, but that is willing to engage in playful ways with alternative possibilities. Thus the "as at first" return to normalcy is not obvious or settled. Surely there were those in Israel who resisted the reemergence of judges as very risky and wished for the stability of kingship; at the same time there were, no doubt, those who remembered the monarchy as predatory and usurpatious, and who wished for the more open ordering of a less regulated society.

None of this in Isaiah and Jeremiah is prescriptive or predictive. I do not cite these texts because they provide clues to our own "return to normalcy;" they do not. Rather, I cite them, because they may suggest to us how a faith tradition may responsibly participate in the debate about what may be "better" that is, how we could "build back better." If we work with these models of a bucolic option of judges and shepherds or with the urban option of kingship, we might consider models available to us from our memory concerning a restored political economy.

When we pursue the *judges-shepherd model* of social organization, we get an image of a simpler ordering of face-to-face neighborliness that is without huge structures of governance, tax collection and military investment. There is an attractiveness to this simplicity. Except that it can never yield the kind of juggernaut of economic, military and technological power that goes with "MAGA" visions of restored greatness. On the other hand, a *model of urban kingship* yields a strong centralized government. Such a government is capable of mustering great resources for wellbeing and security; it is, however, also capable of great monopoly of resources and opportunities for predation for the privileged.

The question of models of normalcy is a tricky and complex one that admits of no obvious settlement. That is why poetic-prophetic work must be done in order to keep before us open-ended possibilities that cannot be closed off by premature ideological conclusions. Indeed, the prophetic voices of the Old Testament are preoccupied with just such imaginings:

- *Isaiah* imagines a future in which the vulnerable are protected:

  With righteousness he shall judge the poor,
    and decide with equity for the meek of the earth;
  He shall strike the earth with the rod of his mouth,
    and with the breath of his lips
    he shall kill the wicked. (Isa 11:3–4).

- *Jeremiah* imagines a welcome embrace of the Torah made possible by forgiveness:

  I will put my law within them, and I will write it on their hearts; and I will be their God, and they shall be my people ... for I will forgive their iniquity, and remember their sin no more. (Jer 31:33–34)

- *Ezekiel* imagines the rule of God deployed on behalf of the vulnerable:

  I myself will be the shepherd of my sheep, and I will make them lie down, says the Lord God. I will seek the lost, and I will bring back the strayed, and I will bind up the injured, and I will strengthen the weak. (Ezek 34:15–16)

- *Amos* imagines a renewed agriculture and a restored urban life:

  The time is surely coming, says the Lord,
    when the one who plows shall overtake the one who reaps,
    and the reaper of grapes the one who sows the seed;
  the mountains shall drip sweet wine,
    and all the hills shall flow with it.
  I will restore the fortunes of my people Israel,
    and they shall rebuild the ruined cities and inhabit them;
  they shall plant vineyards and drink their wine,
    and they shall make gardens and eat their fruit. (Amos 9:13–14)

- *Habakkuk* imagines a tenacious faith for very hard times:

  Though the fig tree does not blossom,
    and no fruit is on the vines;
  though the produce of the olive fails,
    and the fields yield no food;
  though the flock is cut off from the fold,
    and there is no herd in the stalls,
  Yet I will rejoice in the Lord;
  I will exult in the God of my salvation. (Hab 3:17–18)

These poets teem with alternative visions of the new normal.

It is reported that the first apostles asked the risen Christ: "Lord, is this the time when you will restore the kingdom of Israel?" (Acts 1:6). They received no direct answer. It is clear, in any case, that what they hoped for is not what he promised. They hoped for a Davidic restoration; they got from him parables: two coats, two sons, one Samaritan, a mustard seed, images that problematized any simplistic notion of restoration. It is clear in prophetic expectation that restoration is indeed *a gift from God*. It is equally clear, however, that restoration is *a human task*. We are not passive recipients. We may have a decisive say in the shape of the restoration. It is urgent that we exercise intentional agency about that coming future, that we are not caught with a future imposed upon us that is inimical to our common wellbeing. These parabolic offerings of the coming future are tilted toward generosity, forgiveness, compassion, and hospitality, not waylaid by any strident "MAGA." The poets imagine that there will be a time to "build back better." But it will take some sustained intentional doing. This poetic-parabolic future characteristically features fresh human decision-making. That future is not imposed. It can be received but at the same time generated.

15

Snow as Testimony

WE HAD OUR FIRST snow on December 12; five inches. It came beautifully and of course silently. The slowdown and shutdown of Covid invited me to take the snow as an opportunity to reminisce, not unlike Ingmar Bergman's *Wild Strawberries*. I remembered that snow is welcome for the sake of a snowman. I have a photo for my first grade. My dad was about 5 foot, 8 inches; the snowman is a big head taller than my dad. I remembered that snow is useful for snowballs. I remember in the second grade in Hudson, Kansas that the "bigger boys" (likely the fifth graders) kept the girls as hostages pinned down in the school outhouse with snowballs. They stayed there until our principal put a stop to it (I think his name was "Mr. Likleder"). The pelting scenario seemed to me at the time to be a dangerous act of civil disobedience. I remembered that snow is amenable to fast sleds and toboggans. I did that many times down Art Hill in St. Louis with my sons. The trek back up Art Hill to the Art Museum seemed as daunting as Mao's "Long March." I learned, by remembering snowmen, snowballs, and the sled, that snow is a wondrous multi-purposed gift from God; that remains true even if we take into account both the risks of slipping on icy walks or the snarl of bad traffic.

Long before us, however, writers in the Bible also learned that snow is a multi-purposed gift from God. I can identify three texts in which snow is received as testimony to the governance of YHWH. In the exultant poetry of Isaiah 40–55 it is asserted at the outset that, "the word of our God will stand forever" (Isa 40:8). That "word of our God" that is the subject of the poetry concerns the emancipation and restoration of exiled Israel. In sum, that word is "Here is your God" (40:9). Or alternatively, "Your God reigns" (52:7). The "word" is the performative declaration that God's governance and God's emancipatory fidelity are under way, even in the face of Babylonian power and the claims of Babylonian gods (Isa 46:1–2; 47:5–7). The poetry of Isaiah includes doxologies of power (44:24–28), salvation oracles of assurance (41:9–10; 43:1–7), and assaults on Babylonian arrogance (47:1–15).

When the poet wants to add confirming evidence for the reliability of God's emancipatory word, such evidence is not found in historical matters. Rather, the poet must go outside the historical process to appeal to the reliable regularities of creation that the creator guarantees. By the end of this poetry, in chapter 55, the poet finds verification of God's reliable word concerning Israel by an analogue to the reliability of creation:

> For as the rain and the snow come down from heaven,
> and do not return until they have watered the earth,
> making it bring forth and sprout,
> giving seed to the sower and bread to the eater,
> so shall my word be... (Isa 55:10–11).

Rain sent by the creator will not quit until it has watered the earth. Snow dispatched by the creator will not quit until it has caused sprouts that will provide seed and bread. Snow is reliable and does its proper work. Snow is a part of the generative arrangement of creation from the outset:

> As long as the earth endures,
> seedtime and harvest, cold and heat,
> summer and winter, day and night,
> shall not cease. (Gen 8:22)

For Isaiah the purpose of snow is to cause the earth to bring forth. Can you imagine that snow would not water the earth? No, snow is relentless in its purpose. It attests to the reliable order of life-giving processes as willed by the creator.

Thus Isa 55:10 voices the analogue. In 55:11 the poet draws the inference permitted by the snow. The analogue is that God's word is as reliable as is snow. Snow has its proper purpose and will perform it. So also God's word has it proper purpose and will perform it. The purpose of snow (after snowmen, snowballs, and sleds) is to water the earth with the intent of food production. The purpose of God's word in which it will succeed is the restoration of Israel. The poet insists: Look at the snow! You can see there evidence of the reliability of God and God's word. It is evidence from creation that pertains to history. It is evidence that exiled Israel can count on. It is evidence that every needy community and every desperate person can count on. God's word will not fail until it does it purpose. Savor every flake, because every flake bears witness, so claims the poet, to the life-giving reliability of God.

In a very different mode the poet of the book of Job picks up the theme of snow. The reference to snow occurs in a torrent of questions that the creator God puts to Job. Job had imagined that he had reduced the operation of creation to a predictable calculus whereby his deeds would match with certain outcomes. The God hidden in the whirlwind refuses to be trapped in or contained by any such human calculation. For that reason God is determined to show Job that the difference between *human control* through calculation and *God's freedom* is not one of difference of degree, but a difference of kind. In order to assert that vast distinction that is beyond every human capacity or arithmetic process, Job is addressed with questions that do not admit answer, but intend to show Job his penultimate place in the world governed by YHWH.

The questions come at Job with pounding rapidity and without allowance for any response (38:4–37). The required answers are cast as humility:

>Where were you? ... nowhere (v. 4).
>
>Have you commanded? ... no (v. 12).
>
>Have you entered? ...no (v. 16), etc. etc., etc.

So we come to our reference to snow:

>Have you entered the storehouses of the snow
> or have you seen the storehouses of the hail,
>which I have reserved for the time of trouble,
> for the day of battle and war? (Job 37:22–23)

These verses that form a single strophe in the poetry include two questions. The first question in vv. 22–23 asks Job if he has been given access to the great reservoirs of snow and hail over which the creator presides. Of course the required answer is "no." Human persons have been given no access. And just to secure the point, God's speech reminds Job that snow and hail are kept in reserve for times of trouble, battle, and war, because the surprise of snow at any time might tilt the outcome of a battle. (The point might even allow an allusion to the hail that hit Pharaoh (Exod 9:13–35). Job must know that even the military prowess of kings and armies are "at the mercy" of the elements and cannot control them.

The second question in v. 24 asks about source of light and the destiny of the east wind. Of course Job knows nothing more of light and wind than he does of snow and hail. He does not know. He cannot know. He does not know and cannot know because he, as a human knower, is in a world of mighty mystery that evokes wonder but not control.

Thus snow attests to the mighty hidden mystery of God that defies human control. The snow is witness to sovereignty. This claim is of course pre-scientific; or better, it is non-scientific or we may say post-scientific, because after our best reasoning we are left in wonder of a doxological kind.[1] Thus the proverb asserts the scale of difference between the creator who questions and Job who cannot answer:

> It is the glory of God to conceal things,
>   but the glory of kings to search things out. (Prov 25:2)

It is the proper business of science (by kings=government sponsorship) to find out; it is the way of God to conceal. The work of Prometheus goes on; but at least in biblical scope, God's way is not a problem to be solved, but rather a mystery to ponder in awe. The snow testifies to the awesome wonder of God before whom kings may pause, along with Job, to take notice of our penultimate place in God's world.

The aggressive questioning of Job by God is echoed with more restraint by Elihu whose words precede those from the whirlwind. Elihu reports on the stunning wonder he experiences as he witnesses creation:

> At this also my heart trembles,
>   and leaps out of its place. (Job 37:1)

Then follows an inventory of the wonders of creation:

> Under the whole heaven he lets it [thunder] loose,
>   and his lightening to the corners of the earth.
> After it his voice roars;
>   he thunders with his majestic voice
>   and he does not restrain the lightenings when his voice is heard.
> God thunders wondrously with his voice;
>   he does great things that we cannot comprehend.
> For to the snow he says "'Fall on the earth":
>   and the shower of rain, his heavy shower of rain. (vv. 3–6)

---

1. Brown, *The Seven Pillars of Creation*; and Brown, *Wisdom's Wonder*.

The list includes thunder and lightning, snow and rain, all wonders that bespeak God's governance that evokes goose bumps for Elihu. Elihu can only conclude: "He caused it to happen" (v. 13).

It is not a surprise that the poetry of Second Isaiah and Job is echoed (or perhaps anticipated) in the doxological tradition of the Psalms. In the third doxological unit of Psalm 147 (after vv. 1–6 and vv. 7–11) the center of the hymn concerns exactly the wonder of creation:

> He fills you with the finest of wheat.
> He sends out his command to the earth;
> > his word runs swiftly.
> He gives snow like wool;
> > he scatters frost like ashes.
> He hurls down hail like crumbs—
> > who can stand before his cold?
> He sends out his word, and melts them;
> > he makes his wind blow, and the waters flow. (Ps 147:14b–18)

By now these are the usual subjects that attest to God's majestic sovereignty: snow, hail, wind, water.

These are all evocations of Israel's praise. Israel at worship does not explain; it praises; it exults; it celebrates a world that is out beyond human management. Such doxology is ready acknowledgement in Israel concerning the penultimate place of human capacity in creation, a lesson Job was slow to learn. Indeed, it is a lesson that we have been slow to learn as we, in our promethean posturing, imagine that human agency, human freedom, and human technology together constitute the last truth of the world we inhabit. Israel's doxology is a ready affirmation that calls us to recognize our penultimate role in creation.

This doxology does one other remarkable thing. The lines concerning creation in 14b–18 are sandwiched between verses that bespeak Israel's special status in God's attentiveness. In these verses "the Lord" is "Your God, O Zion" (v. 1):

> For he strengthens the bars of your gates;
> > he blesses your children within you.
> He grants peace within your borders . . .
> He declares his word to Jacob,
> > his statues and ordinances to Israel.
> He has not dealt thus with any other nation;
> > they do not know his ordinances.
> Praise the Lord! (Ps 147:13–14a, 19–20).

At its best Israel's doxology is always with a double focus. Such praise readily affirms the chosenness of Israel. This other accent on creation, however, precludes any thought that Israel itself can be the single focus of the creator. The snow attests both YHWH's sovereign generative goodness and Israel's special but qualified place in creation.

Finally we can notice in the next Psalm that even snow is reckoned among God's doxological creatures:

> Let them praise the name of the LORD,
>   for he commanded and they were created.
> He established them forever and ever;
>   he fixed their bounds which cannot be passed.
> Praise the Lord from the earth,
>   you sea monsters and all deeps,
> fire and hail, snow and frost,
>   stormy wind fulfilling his command!
> Mountains and all hills,
>   Fruit trees and all cedars!
> Wild animals and all cattle,
>   creeping things and flying birds! (Ps 148:5–10)

It should not surprise us that snow is alongside both creeping things and kings and princes in praise (see v. 11), because all creatures are in awe, wonder, and gratitude before the creator. Thus we can imagine snow doing its testimony to God's reliability (Isa 55:10–11) and God's unanswerable sovereignty (Job 38), and then gladly returning to the never-ending creaturely doxology in praise alongside many other creaturely companions.

Two things occur to me about this poetry in Second Isaiah and Job. First, these two great poets are both most plausibly dated to the sixth century exile of Israel. If that may for now be assumed, thus the locus for the poetry suggests that when these poets wanted to witness to God's reliability (Isaiah 55) and God's sovereignty (Job), they could not find adequate reference points in history, so failed was their history in the moment. For that reason they had to go outside of history to find persuasive evidence of God's reliability and sovereignty. They appealed to creation to provide resources from which to affirm some truth about history as well, even when history itself is seemingly unreliable and out of control. These two great poets of course had no fear of "natural theology," because they took all of "nature" as a sphere of God's good rule. We ourselves, in our most vexed times, might also appeal to such reliability and sovereignty that live beyond the rush of our control or explanation.

One other matter occurs to me about these poetic offers. Who could have looked at snow and been led to see it as witness to divine reality? Who could have looked at snow and let it evoke confidence in God's ultimacy and awareness of human penultimacy? The ones who could look and see this were the ones who had been steeped in liturgical tradition and schooled in a God-awareness that instructs us in how to see and notice differently. Such God-awareness is worth the effort. Otherwise we may look at snow and see it only for snowmen, snowballs, and fast sleds. These poets know better. We may let their stunning imagination reshape our own capacity to notice differently. We may, with great confidence, trust in their words, gladly saying or singing, "Let it snow, let it snow, let it snow." And for those of you, dear readers, who live in warmer climes where it does not snow, go visit the land of cold beautiful testimony.

16

Solidarity that Counts

SECOND SUNDAY OF EASTER
PSALM 133; ACTS 4:32–35

Psalm 133, the Psalm appointed for the lectionary, offers a compelling vision of a community that is in glad harmony and solidarity. The newer translation, "kindred," amends the older (more familiar and therefore, more convenient) translation of "brothers." The Psalm includes all members of the community in solidarity, all brothers and sisters. This brief poem offers two suggestive images for such social solidarity. On the one hand, "precious oil" (olive oil) is a luxury; but here it is in such abundance that careless wastefulness is in order. Community solidarity is like that, overflowing in celebrative abundance. That is how good community solidarity can be! On the other hand such solidarity is as welcome as dew, reassuring sight on the mountain while the land below is always under threat from draught.

It is possible to read this Psalm as simply a "nice statement" perhaps anticipating Rodney King, who pleadingly asked, "Can't we all just get along?' It is may be like the camaraderie of the Rotary Club without too much required or expected. The Psalm might be no more than generic "thoughts and prayers" that we extend to each other without inconvenience. The Psalm can be read in such a trivializing way. If, however, we pay close attention, we will notice that "kindred" (brothers) is quite expansive and inclusive in the horizon of Israel's Torah. On the one hand we may notice that in Amos 1:9 it is remembered that Israel has a "brotherly"

Solidarity that Counts

"covenant of kinship" with Edom, a notion rooted in the old Jacob-Esau narrative. On the other hand I notice that in the provision for debt cancellation, the "brother" is the target of generosity, most especially the poor brother (Deut 15:1–18):

> Every creditor shall remit the claim that is held against a neighbor, not exacting it of a neighbor who is *a member of the community*, because the LORD's remission has been proclaimed . . . you must remit your claim on whatever any *member of your community* owes you . . . If there is among you anyone in need, *a member of your community* in any of your towns within the land that the LORD your God is giving you, do not be hard-hearted or tight-fisted toward your needy neighbor . . . Be careful that you do not entertain a mean thought . . . and therefore view your needy neighbor with hostility and give nothing . . . If a *member of your community*, either a Hebrew man or a Hebrew woman, is sold to you and works for you six years, in the seventh year you shall set that person free. (Deut 15:2–3, 7, 9, 11–12)

It is important to notice that in this Torah context concerning economic relief, the "brother" who receives relief by the cancellation of debts in the seventh year is the target of generous justice for the sake of the wellbeing of the comity. In the NSRV, the many uses of "brother" are variously translated:

v. 2 brother: The phrase "the brother" is deleted in an editorial judgment;

v. 3 brother = "member of the community";

v. 7. brother = "member of your community";

v. 9 brother: is deleted is a preference to "neighbor";

v. 11 brother = "neighbor";

v. 12 brother = "member of your community."

If we are to understand the gravitas of "brothers together in unity" in the Psalm, then we must see that "brother" is a quite expansive notion, especially when we remember that even the non-Israelite sojourner was a recipient of generosity commanded by the Torah. This awareness of brotherly social solidarity is much more expansive than familial bloodlines, comprehending all those who inhabit common ground. In v. 3 of the psalm, moreover, it is asserted that as a brotherly society Israel is where God has "ordained" a blessing of life forever more.

In Deut 15 concerning debt cancellation, Moses declares:

> There will, however, be no one in need among you, because the LORD is sure to bless you in the land that the LORD your God is giving you as a possession to occupy. (v. 4)

The interface of "brother" and "blessing" in the Psalm is an echo of the Torah assurance. God's blessing is upon the economy of the community when neighborly generosity is practiced. That practice is more than "thoughts and prayers," but concerns active economic engagement on behalf of the wellbeing of all the neighbors through the redress of debt. When the psalm is read in light of the Torah provision of Deut 5:1–18, it is evident that Torah teaching places a weighty mandate upon those *with resources* to make those resources available to those in the community who are *without resources*. Such a mandate, in a covenantal context, requires a significant reformulation of economic guidelines and measurements. The Psalm is thus far from being a "nice" superficiality.

The material dimension of "kin dwelling together in unity" is even more unmistakable when we read this Psalm in the light of the lectionary. It is a happy happenstance that on this Easter Sunday the Psalm is juxtaposed to a reading in the book of Acts that concerns community resources:

> Now the whole group of those who believe were of one heart and soul, and no one claimed private ownership of any possessions, that everything they owned was held in common. (Acts 4:32)

While this simple verse has often been read as "early Christian communism," it need not be read in such a particular way. Rather, with a little evangelical common sense the text portrays a community in which economic resources were willingly shared in common need and glad generosity. This sharing, according to the text, is without any distinct economic theory in play.

In this Easter season it is important to notice that in vv. 32 and 33 our reading juxtaposes *common goods* and *resurrection faith*. The good news of Easter is not some esoteric other worldly secret. It is, rather, the empowerment of the faithful to live differently in the world, differently in a way that refuses our common habits and impulses of greed, and that sees other "members of the community" as those who share and participate in the common resources of the community. It is telling that in Acts 4:34 it is asserted of the early Christian community that "there was not a needy person among them." This verdict is surely an echo of the expectation of Moses noted above that when debts are cancelled, poverty is overcome:

> There will, however, be no one in need among you because the Lord is sure to bless you in the land that the Lord your God is giving you as a possession to occupy. (Deut 15:4)

It is worth notice that this remarkable promissory verse in the mouth of Moses is an important qualification of v. 11 in the same utterance of Moses:

> Since there will never cease to be some in need on the earth, I therefore command you, "open your hand to the poor and needy neighbor in your land." (v. 11)

These two verses together consist in a *realistic acknowledgment of socioeconomic facts on the ground,* and *the Easter mandate* that the faithful may impinge upon socioeconomic reality in transformative ways. And if one has the thought that such radical redefinition of socioeconomic reality is impossible, the church has ready at hand the conviction of resurrection, a claim that plunges us into a new practice of social reality.

This juxtaposition of texts invites the pastors, teachers, and interpreters of the church to serious engagement with the economic crisis that our society faces and the economic challenges that are now on offer. The bold initiative of President Biden in the American Rescue Act Plan suggests that the old rules of individualized parsimony need not be the order of the day, rules that Moses declared to be "hard-hearted" and "tight-fisted" (Deut 15:7). It is neither necessary nor appropriate that church interpreters should be advocates for Biden's policy. But even without such overt advocacy there is ample room for sharing the ways in which faith reasons differently about resources and needs, about brothers and sisters and neighbors, about the stubbornness of poverty, and the Easter prospect of acting differently. It turns out that "kin dwelling together in unity" is not simply a sweet phrase. It is, rather, an evangelical vision of acting differently in policy and practice whereby creditors and debtors share a common social destiny.

The mandates of Easter are not easily convenient. Interpreters of the lectionary reading in Act 4 might legitimately take a peek at the next narrative in Acts 5:1–11, a text that seems deliberately juxtaposed to our lectionary text. In the narrative of Acts 5 Ananias and Sapphira are featured as two members of the community of faith who find the mandates of Easter commonality too demanding and, conversely, found the old habits of private security irresistible. The sin that caused their death was that they cheated on the community by holding back resources from the community.

Their conduct is profoundly in contrast to that of the community members featured in our lectionary text.

It is time in the Easter season of the church in the powerful grip of the resurrection to see that our conventional economics that withholds resources needed by the neighbors is a deathly sin. It is a deathly sin even if it is accepted (since Adam Smith and John Locke) as ordinary practical economic sense. Easter is an opportunity to recognize that our old economic practices are anti-neighborly and have failed. It is a time in the presence of the risen Christ to speak differently about property, possessions, resources, and debt. Imagine: no one in need! The text asserts that there was "great grace upon them all" (Acts 4:33). *Great grace* invites *neighborly generosity* that empowers both local acts of neighborliness and public policies of generosity. There is in fact no other way for "kin to live together in unity."

We may draw these conclusions about the way in which the Easter church thinks about economic resources:

- The Easter church no longer finds our conventional celebration of capitalism to be compelling.
- The Easter church no longer finds dire warnings about socialism to be persuasive.
- The Easter church has no commitment to any abstract ideology of either capitalism or socialism; it is, rather, committed to an economics of neighborliness.

Easter is the good news that God's power for life has defeated death; this is matched by the good news that God's power intends the defeat of poverty. That is how sisters and brothers dwell together in unity, with enough oil for every beard and enough dew for every mountain. This is solidarity that counts resources for the community. When solidarity does not count, it does not matter.

17

The "Ands" of the Gospel

In her remarkable book, *Silver, Sword & Stone: Three Crucibles in the Latin American Story,* Marie Arana summarizes and reviews the tortured (and torturing!) history of Latin America since the arrival of the first Europeans. The three components of her title (that organize her book) make reference in turn to:

"Silver": The passionate ruthless drive for *gold*;

"Sword": an intense readiness for brutal *violence*, and

"Stone": the powerful grip of the *Church* and earlier organized religion as a durable ideological justification for greed.

The story, as is commonly rehearsed, is an account of how European power and greed overwhelmed and domesticated the extant populations of Latin America. This power established the rule of greed, put in place in the sixteenth century that remains largely intact and in effect today.

On the final page of her book, Arana notes that we have largely seen Latin American history "from the eye of the invader, from the perspective of conquest" which has produced "a long litany of iniquities [that] lie at the heart of the Latin American narrative."[1] Against that European bias Arana insists that we must pay greater attention to the indigenous culture and history, so that must be a study of "ands":

> The story of Columbus *and* the Taino. The story of Cortes *and* . . . the Aztecs. Pizzaro . . . *and* the Incas. Cabeza de Vaca *and* the

---

1. Arana, *Silver, Sword & Stone*, 362.

Guarani. Spain *and* its colonies. The tinpot dictator *and* his unfortunate casualties. The Roman Catholic Church *and* the pagans. The vast world economy *and* the coveted veins that lie dormant in the earth.[2]

Having stated the "ands," Arana goes on to insist:

> But it is the "*ands*," the second parties to each dyad, that reveal the underlying and often more enduring aspects of the story: it is the Taino, the Aztec, the Inca, the Guarani, the colonies, the pagans, the casualties, and the veins that lie dormant in the earth that tell the deeper tale. These are the constituent parts that, however trampled, remain deeply imprinted on the region's psyche.

Strong ideological forces have led us to disregard and downplay the second part of the "ands." Now required is a rediscovery and new appreciation of the parts of the "ands" that we have not noticed.

Arana's accent on the "ands" has led me to think about the "ands" of the gospel that require a rereading of faith. In what follows I consider some of those "ands" that have occurred to me while readers may think of many others. From the Old Testament here are three such "ands" that strike me as important:

1. *Israelite and Canaanite.* Our wont is to follow the dominant storyline of the biblical text and focus singularly on Israel with hardly an afterthought about the Canaanites. Even if we took the simple claim that Israel displaced the Canaanites, we are still left with the fact of displaced people that lingered in the memory of Israel as a result of ideological violence. But of course the Bible, in addition to the story of wholesale displacement, also acknowledges that the "conquest" was not as clean and absolute as that. In Judges 1, it is reiterated that Israel "did not drive out" the Canaanites. They remained in the land. They continued to exist as a very distinct population.

Thus even given the powerful ideology of a "chosen people" who were "given the land of promise," the text bears witness to the fact that "other people" with their own claim to the land are present in the biblical text. These "other people" in the text function variously as a threat to the faith and as a resource for faith and culture; Israel obviously borrowed very much from the Canaanites. The notion of a "clean sweep" of the land, moreover, has served well the Euro-American narrative that the early "American settlers" came to a land that was eagerly received and necessarily made "empty" of

---

2. Arana, *Silver, Sword & Stone*, 362.

its early population. Of course the facts are very different, for the memory and the continuing presence of an "unwelcome" population can only be denied in and through an illusionary ideology. That unwelcome population cannot be denied by Euro-Americans concerning Native Americans, any more than Israelis can persuasively deny the continuing reality of a Palestinian community with its own claim to the land. The "and" of "us" and "other" requires much greater attention than a singular ideology of chosenness has permitted, both in the Bible and in the U.S. cultural history that is dominated by Euro-American notions of "superiority." It is the "others" who come after the "and" that insist on greater attention and appreciation.

2. *Israelite and sojourner*. In the Bible sojourners are those who lived among the Israelites but who were without tribal membership and who were therefore vulnerable and without social protection. In the same chapter of Leviticus where we find "the second great commandment" ("You shall love your neighbor as yourself"; Lev 19:18; see Mark 12:31), we get another startling commandment:

> When an alien resides with you in your land, you shall not oppress the alien. The alien who resides with you shall be to you as the citizen among you; you shall love the alien as yourself, for you were aliens in the land of Egypt; I am the LORD your God. (Lev 19:33–34)

The community of Israel was never to be "a pure community" consisting only in its own kind. It has always had to deal with "outsiders" who did not "belong." It was easy enough, given the ideology of chosenness, to dismiss the presence and claim of the "non-eligible others." The text, however, would not permit such exclusivism or dismissal of the other. Not only does the commandment preclude oppression of the other; it mandates "love" for the sojourner as for self, the same formulation as for the neighbor in the better known v. 18. The mandate for such generous policy and practice is the memory of Israel as vulnerable sojourners amid Egyptian oppression.

The point is made clear in Exod 12:48–49 in which a sojourner is admitted to the Passover celebration, and so is given access to Israel's narrative of emancipation: "There shall be one law (*torah*) for the native and for the alien who resides among you" (v. 49). Israel could never be without the "other." It is easy to see what happens when the subject after the "and" is eliminated from the horizon of the chosen. Then the claim of Israel can become exclusionary and can deny to the other both dignity and security. The subject after the "and" keeps Israelite exclusionary passion in check. When the matter is taken more generally the "and" precludes racist superiority, and any illusion that "we" are the only ones there, or the only ones who have legitimate rights and claims.

3. *Wolf and lamb.* The remarkable anticipatory oracle of Isaiah presents a series of "and" pairs:

> Wolf and lamb,
>
> leopard and kid,
>
> calf and lion,
>
> cow and bear,
>
> lion and ox,
>
> nursing child and asp,
>
> weaned child and adder. (Isa 11:6–8)

In each pair one member is an aggressive predator; the other in each case is a vulnerable subject as potential prey. The prophet, however, imagines a creation that is fully reconciled in which the strong and the weak, predator and prey, are fully at peace with each other. Without the "and" we might imagine a world in which predators prevail and the more exposed subjects live in endless vulnerability until they are devoured or destroyed. That presumed world, in the horizon of the poet, however, has no future. It has no future because the "spirit of the Lord" will be embodied in actual governance marked by righteousness, equity, and faithfulness. The outcome of this poetic anticipation is an absence of hurt. The insistence on the "and" is a guarantee that we will not accept the premise of predator/prey as "normal." Such a practice, wherever it occurs, is recognized as quite abnormal and without sustaining power.

These three cases of "and,"

> Israelite and Canaanite,
>
> Israelite (citizen) and sojourner,
>
> wolf and lamb

bespeak a world that refuses ideological closure and any simple reductionism. The insistence on the pairs keeps open the socioeconomic possibility for every creature present. Any attempt to erase this presence is a violation of Torah.

The matter of course is not different in the New Testament. I deem the triadic formulation of Gal 3:28 to be the richest "and" text in the tradition.

The "Ands" of the Gospel

The struggle for Paul in his letters to the Romans and the Galatians is how Jewish Christians who keep Torah *and* Gentile Christians who do not keep Torah can live together in community. In Gal 3:28, to be sure, the specific formulation is "no longer, no longer, no longer." The point, however, is that the gospel community is always both/and, because both parties belong to, are claimed by, and welcomed by Christ. Both parties before and after the "and" are heirs to the promises of Abraham.

1. *There is no longer Jew or Greek.* There is both Jew and Greek. The struggle in the early church was whether Gentile Christians who did not keep Torah would be first class members. Paul is unwavering in his advocacy of inclusion that would readily challenge the priority of Jewish Christians who kept Torah. The point of torah-keeping is for Paul a non-issue, because the overwhelming reality of the gracious governance of Christ overrides all such distinctions. From the outset the church has always been busy trying to sort out such distinctions and to establish orders or hierarchies of authority, privilege, or entitlement. Against such seductions, Paul asserts a non-discriminatory "and" that refuses all such classification. The church community includes both Jews and Gentiles. Gentiles cannot be lopped off after the "and."

2. *Free and slave.* Slavery was a long practiced socioeconomic arrangement in Paul's world as it continues to be in the modern world. The issue of slavery is even more acute in the US economy because of the additional factor of race. At base, slavery is an assumption that some are more properly assigned to hard labor and others are certified to the ease and surplus produced by that hard labor. Beneficiaries of such arrangements go to great lengths to dress up and justify that duality in all kinds of ways, but basically it is a cultural-economic insistence that some are entitled and some are not. Paul is unconvinced: not so in Christ! Not so in the ancient world where Paul lives. Not so in the contemporary world of huge economic inequality. Not so in the present surge of white supremacy among us. Not so amid our pathology concerning immigration. Not so in the world of sex trafficking. Not so, because the truth of the gospel has demolished all such self-serving arrangements and all such economic incongruities. In Christian community, it is both slave *and* free, both creditors *and* debtors, both those long privileged *and* those long subjugated. Whenever the church participates in those old dismissive distinctions it transgresses its true nature and the will of its Lord. Paul's insistence is uncompromising.

3. *Male and female.* Much like us, Paul lived in a world where male privilege and male authority were well established and taken as normal.

Indeed, much of society continues to be a "male only" enterprise without any "and." But not so in Christ! In the gospel it is always male and female, or better, female and male. Thus there is in the gospel as voiced by Paul an insistence on gender equity. Richard Hayes has it just right:

> Paul is echoing the language of Gen. 1:27: "*male and female* he created them." To say that this created distinction is no longer in force is to declare that the new creation has come upon us, a new creation in which gender roles no longer pertain.[3]

(It is curious that Hayes elsewhere still allows the statement of Rom 1:26–27 to trump this claim when it comes to LGBTQ persons.) I have no doubt that in gospel vision that the "and" of Paul extends to all such persons.

Mary McGann, *The Meal that Reconnects: Eucharistic Eating and the Global Food Crisis*, shows that the table practices of the early church parallel the triad that Paul asserts:

> Inclusive table practices were serious challenges to the hierarchical structures and inequalities of Roman society; Christian slaves, freedmen, and slave owners reclined together; men, women, Jew, Greek, and Gentile shared food. Viewed as a new world order by gathered Christ-followers, these customs would have been judged by local Roman agents as seriously disordered practices.[4]

It is the case, of course, that the "and" that Moses taught and Jesus performed and entrusted to his followers has often been distorted and interrupted. It seems evident that such distortion and interruption happen whenever there is a claim of privilege, entitlement, or chosenness. The claim of chosenness, unless it is seriously circumscribed, will every time lead to a distortion of the "and" of the gospel.[5] We are able to observe such distortion and disruption of the "and"

- in the chosenness of Jews;
- in the chosenness of Christians;
- in the chosenness of Americans, and
- in the chosenness of whites.

---

3. Hays, *Letter to the Galatians*, 273.
4. McGann, *Meal that Reconnects*, 50.
5. See Brueggemann, *Chosen: Reading the Bible amind the Israeli–Palestinian Conflict*.

The "Ands" of the Gospel

It is the critical work of the church to expose all such distortions of the "and" of the gospel. It is the further work of the church to bear witness to and to embody a community of "and" that can and will effectively embrace both,

- Jew and Greek,
- Free and slave,
- Male and female.

This accent upon the "and" of the gospel has immense implication amid our economic inequality, our racist assumptions, and our pathological fear of immigrants. Indeed, this "and" touches every great issue that is before our public body.

The enduring tradition of "ands" is made possible and urgent for Paul because of his expansive conviction about the Abrahamic tradition that is a free gift of God's promise. With Abraham, God has initiated a *novum* in human history. All the later attempts to draw lines of exclusion are futile because the promise to Abraham is broad, deep, and unconditional. For good reason Paul can assert about the God of Abraham that he is,

> The God in whom he believed, who gives life to the dead and calls into existence the things that do not exist. (Rom 4:17)

As a consequence, the embrace of "and" extends as far as Paul is able to imagine.

It is surely the case, as Arana judges, that we will not grasp the import of the history and culture of Latin America until we pay close attention to the "second parties to each dyad." Our work in faith now is to pay attention to the second half of the dyads . . . Greeks, slaves, females . . . and all the others who are easily dismissed after the preposition. Arana concludes concerning Latin America,

> Until Latin America understands how it people have been shaped, sharpened, and stunted by those iniquities, the crucibles of silver, sword, and stone will continue to write its story.[6]

Matters are not different beyond Latin America where most of us live. We also have a narrative of *silver*, *sword*, and *stone*. Our work is to tell another story of our common life that is not defined by or contained in *gold*, *violence*, or *ideology*. In order to tell that other story, we must attend closely to the "second parties to each dyad."

---

6. Arana, *Silver, Sword & Stone*, 362.

18

The Conditions from Which the Poems Arose

In my exposition, "Refusing Erasure" (Chap. 13 above), I have referred to Carolyn Forché and her book, *What You Have Heard Is True: A Memoir of Witness and Resistance*. The book is her account of the way in which the wise, sly champion of social justice, Leonel Gómez Vides, had "recruited" her to come to El Salvador in order that she can bear witness to the corrupt violence of his society. Vides wanted Forché to come see, because she is a poet and perhaps a poet could bear effective witness to his unbearable social reality. He chastened her by saying, "You can't just write poetry about yourself." He urged her on, saying, "If you are going to be a poet, you must see the world." Her narrative report chronicles the way in which her exposure to El Salvador and its violence made her a very different kind of poet, just as Vides had anticipated. One can see in her new collection of poems, *In the Lateness of the World*, the impact of her time with Gómez Vides in El Salvador.

Forché did not have an easy time at the outset, understanding the political, historical context of El Salvador that surely supplied "the conditions from which the poems arose." I have pondered that phrasing about the condition from which poetry arises, and have concluded that good, serious poetry arises in *contexts of extremity* where prose articulations are inadequate. The "extremity" to which Forché bears witness in her poetry is the great brutality of El Salvador, brutality undertaken by both the government and by numerous guerilla forces.

The Conditions from Which the Poems Arose

I have no expertise concerning poetry, but I have the following notion about it. Good serious poetry is not about rhyme or meter or loveliness. I suggest rather it is daringly marked by:

- *Thickness.* This means it is bottomless in its significance, so that it cannot be exhausted at first hearing or confidently decoded at first glance. It is an offer of words that always evoke further attentiveness, a gift that keeps on giving.

- *Elusiveness:* This means it is filled with swirls of playful possibilities, so that different listeners will receive from it different significations, none of which can prevail, dominate, or grant certitude.

- *Imagistic Richness.* This means it appeals to the concrete quotidian realities of ordinary life. It permits each listener to evoke and trace out, and so to imagine worlds other than the one immediately in front of the listener.

On all counts, poetry then is an enemy of certitude and single meaning, thus refusing, resisting, and subverting the certitude of every claim. The work of poetry is so urgent and so difficult precisely because circumstances of extremity evoke a craving for certitude. Poetry thus becomes an invitation to live, ever more daringly into the extremity, to embrace the freedom required in the extremity, and to accept responsibility for engaging the extremity of risk and danger.

With that in mind I am reminded that the Old Testament is, to a great extent, a book of poetry because it brings its reading community close to *the extremity of a God* who refuses to be boxed in by conventional expectation or reduced to conventional formulation. This is evident in the great poetic offers of Job, Psalms, and Proverbs, but no less so in the great prophetic books. And even in the narrative accounts of the Pentateuch and the "history," poems are strewn here and there at especially poignant pivot points in the telling. In what follows, I will consider two poems embedded in Israel's narrative recital and two poems that are representative of the tradition of the book of Psalms, Israel's most forthright poetic voicing.

Exodus 15:21: *The extremity of emancipation.* This two line poem on the lips of Miriam is perhaps the oldest Israelite poem. It comes at the culmination of the inscrutable emancipation from Pharaoh's brutal slavery. The exodus narrative begins with the "cry and groan" of the slaves (2:23–24). Now it ends in a celebrative dance of freedom as the women articulate with their bodies what it feels like to be out from under the insatiable brick quotas of Pharaoh.

The poem/song is addressed to YHWH. This is the new God who had heard the cry and groan of the slaves and acted for Israel's freedom (Exodus 24–25; 3:7–9). This is a God not known heretofore in Israel. Indeed, this God is not only unknown, but so enigmatic, so beyond human decipherment that this divine name has no vowels and remains unpronounceable (see 3:14). The women who dance and sing their freedom accept this "coded" God as is, and bear witness to the wondrous outcome of divine action.

Like most hymns in Israel, this one begins with an imperative summons to songs of praise. The imperative is followed by an explanatory clause introduced by "for" that gives the reason for songs of praise. The reason here is that YHWH is lifted up in power, might, and wonder. The second line provides concrete imagery that supports the imperative. The poem imagines mighty Pharaoh on his horse riding into the chaotic waters of the Red Sea; or perhaps it is Pharaoh's army; either way, the victory of YHWH is made specific and concrete. The way in which Pharaoh is "dehorsed" is that YHWH has ridden into the chaotic waters and has pushed Pharaoh off his horse to drown. Such imagery of course is a bit too concrete for most theology. But this is poetry! It wants to make divine power as concrete and as immediately available as possible. This is a God, so says the poet, who engages in the specific reality of historical power. Pharaoh is very big on horses, chariots, and other tools of war (Exod 14:23); but he is not big enough. Not powerful enough. Not big or powerful enough to resist the force of freedom caused by this God of emancipation.

Later on, Moses, Miriam's brother, will expand the imagery of the drowning of Pharaoh (Exod 15:4–8). In that derivative poem you can hear Pharaoh gasping for air! We may imagine this "warrior God" reached from his horse to hold Pharaoh under the water until dead. The emancipated slaves have been singing songs and poems to YHWH since then, still singing and dancing freedom. If we look closely at the dead Pharaoh, we might be able to see, as the poem is transported, that it is in fact belatedly Mussolini hung by his toes in Rome, or Nicolae Ceausescu in Romania shot by a firing squad, or any other enemy of freedom who finally could not finally prevail in the world where YHWH presides. The emancipated have continued to sing poems of praise to YHWH since then, still singing and dancing freedom all the way to the fall of the Berlin Wall. Singing and dancing because this indecipherable God of freedom is faithfully at work.

The Conditions from Which the Poems Arose

Second Samuel 1:19–27: *The extremity of grief.* Jonathan, son of King Saul, was heir apparent to the throne of Israel. In his deep devotion to David, however, he ceded his royal claim to David. He fought with his father against the Philistines, until he, alongside his father, was killed in battle (1 Sam 31:2). In response David, in this poem, grieves deeply. The imagery for Jonathan marks him as "swifter than an eagle, stronger than a lion (2 Sam 1:23). Jonathan was not only strong and swift; he is "beloved and lovely":

> Greatly beloved were you to me;
> your love to me was wonderful,
> passing the love of a woman. (v. 26)

The work of grief requires naming and characterizing the lost one. For all of his speed, strength, and loveliness, the accent is on Jonathan's might (*gbr*). Grief work is repetitious, said over and over. So David in his grief will reiterate in vv. 25 and 27: "How the mighty have fallen!"

The death of the beloved prince in Israel is unbearable. It humiliates Israel. Don't report the death! Don't give the Philistines occasion to gloat. Be quiet about his death. The words urge to silence. So we get personal loss plus a concern for public reality. The grief concerns a lovely, well loved man. At the same time, this thick poem invites us to host a great company of the lost who have been well loved. When I read it I thought it referred to John F. Kennedy, lovely and beloved, killed in a way that shattered national wellbeing, as did the death of Jonathan. But now today, as I write this and consider who it might be who is slain and grieved, I thought it was Police Officer Brian Sicknick, the one killed in the DC insurrection of January 6, 2021. His family remembers him as a hero. Do not report his violent death in Gath or in Ashkelon or in any Philistine city; do not let the Philistines gloat. Officer Sicknick was indeed violently killed by "the Philistines" of our time. Do not let the Russians or the Chinese know how we in the United States are in ignominious disarray. David sang for Jonathan; Israel sang for its prince. We, after Israel, sing of loss and our shattered social possibility, as we take Sicknick as a sign of the failure of our social order. The mighty have fallen! They have fallen and continue to fall, because "the Philistines" always have their day. David grieves. And then in the next verses he is made king (2 Sam 2:1–4). This is the story line of human possibility amid savage loss:

- Thus John F. Kennedy was killed—the mighty fallen!—and Lyndon B. Johnson promptly enacted powerful, demanding legislation in his name that ran well beyond Kennedy's own vision.
- Thus Officer Sicknick was violently killed by marauding Philistines—the mighty fallen!—and perhaps Joe Biden will promptly govern with emancipatory vigor and resolve.

In the book of Psalms we may readily identify the two extremities of awe, *praise, wonder and thanks* and *loss, sadness, anger, and rage*. Comment on any hymn in the Psalter can represent the first extremity, and discussion of any lament-complaint in the book of Psalms will give voice to the second extremity.

Psalm 100: *The extremity of awe, praise, wonder, and thanks.* I have selected this Psalm as the most obvious and familiar case in point, the one that is referenced in the "doxology" sung in many churches. This poem is a summons to recognize and acknowledge, by a joyful noise, by gladness, and by singing, that YHWH, the undecipherable God, is Lord of creation and of history. The poem seems to assume that YHWH is made more fully and is recognized more broadly as sovereign by the active engagement of worshiping Israel. Such praise is designed to enhance and magnify YHWH.

As a follow-up to the three-fold summons, the Psalm affirms exactly who YHWH is known to be:

> YHWH is God! YHWH, unlike all other would-be competing gods, has a claim to both power and fidelity. Evidence of YHWH's governance is that he made "us," that is, Israel. Israel is the sheep; YHWH is the good shepherd. This poetry is a means whereby worshiping Israel makes clear both its own identity and the identity of YHWH. (v. 3)

In v. 4, the Psalm extends a second doxological trope. Again the Psalm summons with imperatives: "Enter, give thanks, bless." This triad is a glad, ready affirmation of who YHWH is. Verse 5, introduced by "for," provides ground for thanks. The triad affirms that YHWH, is *good, practices steadfast love*, and *remains faithful*. Thus in a two-fold pattern, we get imperatives and reasons for imperatives. Two images dominate the poetry. First, we get sheep-shepherd, a conventional image for kingship, but given particular substance in the familiar poem of Psalm 23, in the discourse of John 10:7–18, and in the inventory of Ezekiel 34:

> I will seek the lost, and I will bring back the strayed, and I will bind up the injured, and I will strengthen the weak, but the fat and the strong I will destroy. I will feed them with justice. (Ezek 34:16)

The second image is of a liturgical procession of "coming in" and "entering," in gladness into the presence of God. Israel is "on the move" toward YHWH's governance.

The thickness of this poem is evident in our capacity to reuse the Psalm over and over to fund our ongoing celebrative worship. The elusiveness of the poem is unmistakable in that the sheep-shepherd imagery is open to rich imaginative possibility. In the end, the sung poetry of Israel is fixed on the steadfast love and faithfulness of YHWH; this word pair in 100:5 most fully mark YHWH and YHWH's governance. Indeed this word pair from v. 5 is the most elemental claim of Israel's faith. Israel returns to that word pair again and again:

> The LORD, the LORD,
> a God merciful and gracious, slow to anger,
> abounding in *steadfast love* and *faithfulness*. (Exod 34:6)

> But you, O LORD, are a God merciful and gracious,
>   slow to anger and abounding in *steadfast love* and *faithfulness*.
> (Ps 86:15)

> Righteousness and justice are the foundation of your throne;
>   *steadfast love* and *faithfulness* go before you. (Ps 89:14, 33)

These two marks of fidelity distinguish YHWH from all other gods; Israel can never finish singing this. Israel can never stop poetry-making around this singular affirmation.

Psalm 58: *The extremity of loss, sadness, anger, and rage.* Because Israel's faith lives in the real world, it knows from day to day that the threat of chaos does not remain toned down and docile, even given the steadfast love of YHWH. In its singing Israel knows about big trouble! In this Psalm the trouble is from the "wicked" who are cast in despicable imagery:

> They have venom like the venom of a serpent,
>   like the deaf adder that stops its ears (v. 4).

This Psalm of extremity holds nothing back of deep outrage, for this is the God from whom no secret can be hid. The rage against the wicked cannot be hid. The deep revulsion at evil cannot be hid. The hope of brutal vengeance cannot be hid.

The poem begins in wonderment about whether God is morally reliable (v. 1). There is so much concrete evidence to the contrary. Nevertheless, the poem dares to issue imperatives to God on the bet that God has both the will and the capacity to right the wrong and to abuse the wicked in a way commensurate with their destructive action. The first imperatives are direct:

> Break their teeth in their mouths;
> Tear out the fangs of the young lions. (v. 6)

These are followed by jussives that amount to imperatives:

> Let them vanish like water . . .
> like grass let them be trodden down . . .
> Let them be like the snail that dissolves into slime. (vv. 7–8)

That should finish them! This last image has to be among the best in scripture!

The Psalm is framed in confident expectation of God's righteousness against violence (vv. 1–2, 10–11). In between, however, the poet goes "down and dirty" in vengeance and retaliation. Israel knows that the capacity to live in covenantal faithfulness requires truth-telling from the depth of trouble. Israel does not flinch from offensive expression. It has no fear of offending God, because it knows that denial in piety is a non-starter. Consequently, in the book of Psalms we get a torrent of emotive extravagance, all uttered in hope-filled expectation.

These four examples of poetry are sufficient to suggest that covenantal faith in the Bible is designed exactly to submit the extremities of life to the sovereignty of God. But these extremities cannot be "submitted" unless they are brought to honest, specific, daring speech. We are able to see that these several poems are indeed:

Thick in a way that requires continuing attentiveness;

Elusive so that we can appeal to them in many different circumstances, and

Imagistic so that we can readily picture the scenes of awe and rage.

This poetic legacy has been entrusted to the church along with other communities of faith. The church, however, has a strong durable itch toward

The Conditions from Which the Poems Arose

prose. As a result, the playful poetry of the Bible and the thick, elusive, imagistic voice of the gospel get flattened, in practice, into a pattern of certitude. Among progressives such reduction comes down to *Enlightenment rationality* which screens out much of what matters for the gospel. Conversely among fundamentalists there is the same reduction into *scholasticism* and a refusal of what is given as playful in the gospel. (Tellingly enough, a vigorous protest against such fundamentalist reductionism is termed, by its advocates, "Open theism.") The outcome of this twin reductionism is that:

- *the great epic hymns* are brought down to "praise hymns" of seven words eleven times (7/11!), or to romantic ballad-like assurances;
- *the great lyrical prayers* become grocery lists for delivery by God,
- *the great courageous proclamations* are reduced to clever storytelling or earnest moralism.

What a loss! What an abdication shared across the spectrum of church practice!

In such circumstance, we may ask with Forché, "What are the conditions in which poetry emerges?" And the answer is, poetry emerges in extremity,

that *refuses thinness* that is unpersuasive,

that *rejects certitudes* that issue in denial, and

that *shuns well-ordered didacticism* that knows everything ahead of time.

It may be no wonder, given these choices, that the church has failed in its missional witness and become a bulwark for keeping things as they are.

In such a circumstance we may, in quite specific ways, reframe and reconsider that the "meeting space" of the worshiping congregation is an arena for poetic practice that responds to our unmistakable "condition of extremity." In such reframing, we might dare to give voice to

the extremity of emancipation (as with Miriam);

the extremity of grief (as with David);

the extremity of praise (as with Psalm 100 and the hymns of the Psalter); and

the extremity of insistent anger (as with Psalm 58 and the laments of the Psalter).

Such a reframing might evoke a bit of vertigo in the congregation, leave us off balance or at least out of our comfort zone. But those who turn out to be the faithful carriers of the gospel are characteristically more than a little off balance, blown by the wind where they had never thought they would go.

- Imagine these poets in conversation with each other.
- Imagine what Miriam would want to say to David who grieves. She might affirm to the weeping king, "There can be a way out of no way."
- Imagine what David might want to say to Miriam amid her dancing. He might say, "Yes, there will be a way out of no way, but we will nevertheless notice a mighty loss on the way."

We are surely in a condition of extremity, a condition wherein poetry may again arise.

19

The McCarthy Cousins

WITH THE RISE OF Kevin McCarthy to minority leader in the US House of Representatives, I have been thinking about a roster of McCarthys who have crossed our paths in public life. (Because I grew up in a rural community of German immigrants, I never knew anyone named McCarthy, or anyone with any name that sounded like that.) There have been a number of McCarthys in our public life, including Eugene McCarthy, the somewhat quixotic Minnesota senator who boldly forced Lyndon Johnson out of the presidential race in 1968. Here I will consider only three McCarthys, to the disregard of many others.

CHARLIE McCARTHY

While some younger people may not recognize his name, anyone a bit older will happily remember that he was a puppet of Edgar Bergen who thrived in vaudeville and on radio for a very long time. Charlie was something of a smart-ass and enjoyed dialogic engagement with a number of celebrities including Mae West, Dale Evans, and W. C. Fields. Bergen was a quite successful showman and ventriloquist; he was much better on radio than on TV, because he made no secret of moving his lips when he gave voice to Charlie.

The defining feature of Charlie's life was that he was a "dummy." He had no life of his own and no true self. Most important, he had no voice of his own. Bergen was able to put words into his mouth and he spoke them obediently and unerringly. He did so to the delighted entertainment of many of us in my growing up years. I must admit that I appreciated his companion dummy, Mortimer Snerd, even more. We were (and are) easily beguiled and entertained by dummies who speak words other than their own (see Kukla, Fran, and Ollie!).

JOE McCARTHY

The nefarious Republican from Wisconsin was a US senator from 1947 to 1957 when he finished in disgrace. He was and remained an undistinguished legislator until he latched on to the post-war "scare" about "communism," a scare that he was able to elevate to a high art. In his high days of national attention he claimed to have evidence of communists in the government including both General George Marshall and President Eisenhower. Of course he never produced any evidence for such treason; he kept his claimed evidence securely concealed "here in my briefcase." And because we could see his briefcase, the evidence seemed viable, convincing and accessible to us concerning "enemies within" that threatened our democracy. Except that it was none of those, not visible, not convincing, and not accessible. He was, however, capable of transposing innuendo for a time into a political force that threatened and intimated many public persons. His demagoguery proved for a time to be most effective, as many public figures either supported him, or in their cowardice refused to challenge him concerning his unsubstantiated and unsupportable claims. My first exposure to television as a student at Elmhurst College was for the "McCarthy hearings." Our beloved history teacher, Paul Crusius, allowed us to use class time to watch the hearings because he understood them to be politically and historically significant. And indeed they are of continuing significance, for they are a primary example of the way in which democracy can be transposed into obscene political theater.

McCarthy prospered politically for a time while many other political figures at least tacitly colluded with him. His popularity lasted until later, finally, some screwed up their courage and challenged him, exposing him as a fraud. That effort at exposure was led by Senator Margaret Chase Smith of Maine. Happily that exposure brought a swift end to him; but that exposure did not produce a big roster of "Profiles in Courage." His performance success made clear how vulnerable our democracy is to demagoguery that has no restraint for truth-telling.

McCarthy was said to be in private a likeable, normal guy. When he went public, however, he assumed a very different persona and spoke in a very different idiom. His voice was low, ponderous, and gravelly, perhaps to claim some gravitas for his fake claims. His voice of accusation was no normal human voice, but one derived from ideology and expressed through insistent demagoguery. This public self-presentation allowed for the voice of ideology that had no respect for the truth or for conventional norms of political civility. This false voice of ideology in which McCarthy did his character assassination proved most compelling for many people. For many who knew better, his work proved to be convenient and useful for nefarious ends of their own. The dramatic collapse of McCarthy and his "crusade" came in a dramatic senate hearing when a pixie-like lawyer, Joseph Welch, asked him in front of the cameras: "Have you no sense of decency, senator, at long last? Have you left no sense of decency?" The answer to that question, made abundantly clear, was that Joe McCarthy had no sense of decency. His lack of decency led him to give voice to untruth and to play to paranoia and an imagined conspiracy that had no basis in fact, but depended upon phony charges and mean-spirited accusations that could mobilize public opinion in fear. As a result, he did damage to some of the most respected persons in public life. A durable outcome of his charade is that his name has been reduced to an "ism," McCarthyism. Nobody wants his or her name reduced to an "ism"! But so it is for this senator in a dramatic, pathos-filled moment in US history.

KEVIN McCARTHY

As the minority leader in the US House of Representatives, two factors seem important for Kevin McCarthy. One is that he lusts in deep, transparent ways to become Speaker of the House. The other is that his Republican caucus is notoriously unmanageable, as both John Boehner and Paul Ryan have learned. These two factors together require Kevin McCarthy to be inventively agile in managing his caucus, and equally inventive about his drive to become Speaker. It becomes clear as we observe McCarthy's agility that he has not as yet settled on a reliable voice through which to exercise leadership. Thus he can on the one hand acknowledge that Donald Trump bears responsibility for the insurrection of January 6 and its violence. But on another day he can glibly assert that "we are all responsible." He can say that Marjorie Taylor Greene does not represent the GOP norms in the House, but then go to careful lengths to include her in the Republican caucus as an (he hopes) assured vote for his leadership. He flew to Mar-a-Lago for support; and yet had been rebuffed by Trump during the Capitol insurrection. The outcome is a highly volatile leader who has no reliable voice, seeking to be "all things to all people" in a most remarkable and dishonest way. All of that is an attempt to advance his claim to power and influence.

COMPARISON

These three McCarthys are very different from each other:

- Charlie was a dummy who had no voice of his own.
- Joe was no dummy, but he settled on a voice of conspiratorial demagoguery that had no connection to reality.
- Kevin, in his cynicism, has no settled identifiable voice, but he keeps many different voices operative in his opportunistic thirst for power.

These three McCarthy's are not very different about their voices:

- No voice at all;
- The voice of demagoguery;
- No settled voice, a fake trumpet, a fake cadence.

They are, moreover, all related to a practice of secrecy. Edgar Bergen tried to keep secret his lip movement but his lips moved anyway. Joe kept his list of traitors secret in his briefcase, never opening the roster. Kevin is all out in the open with his unconcealed opportunism, hoping only to keep secret his unmistakable self-contradiction. Not one of them has arrived at a capacity for truth-telling, *not Charlie* because he never got to decide, *not Joe* because he was bereft of principle, and *not Kevin* because he wants to keep his options open.

There is in scripture, as far as I know, no direct response to these various McCarthys. I did however think of these texts that seem pertinent. First, Isaiah mocks the careless speaking practices of Jerusalem's leadership (Isa 28:11–16). God has promised rest and repose (v. 11). But the mindless chant of the leaders is to the contrary:

> Do this, do that, do this, do that, rule on rule, rule on rule, a little more, a little more.[1]

---

1. Tull, *Isaiah 1–39*, 423.

That is, such talk is non-committal gibberish. For such speech they can only "fall backward" (v. 13). These "scoffers" have made a "covenant with death," in this case, a covenant with the Assyrians who will invade the city (vv. 15, 18). In the end, says the prophet, God will counter this stammering company with fresh initiatives of steadfastness, righteousness, and justice (vv. 16–17).

In his famous temple sermon, Jeremiah reprimands the leaders of Jerusalem who engage in pious liturgic chatter:

> Do not trust in these deceptive words: "This is the temple of the LORD, the temple of the LORD, the temple of the LORD." (7:4)

Such a popular mantra is perhaps not unlike the often reiterated slogans of patriotism among us today. Jeremiah saw that such piety simply provided cover for actions and policies that violated neighborly covenant. All the while, during such recitals, they

> steal, murder, commit adultery, swear falsely, make offering to Baal, and go after other gods that you have not known. (7:9)

Their end, says the prophet, can only be a complete obliteration, not unlike that of Shiloh centuries before (vv. 14–15). Empty talk serves no useful purpose and one must not be misguided by such utterance, not by a puppet, not by a *demagogue*, and not by an *opportunist*.

If we juxtapose these three McCarthys and their failed speech with the statements of Isaiah and Jeremiah about such phony speech we can draw a conclusion that pertains to our public matters. It matters if such speech is phony. It matters if such speech is demagogic. The prophetic alternative to such speech is truth-telling that pertains to the rule of God which is not allied with any ideology; such speech concerning the rule of God, moreover, is characteristically speech about the common good, about neighborly good that embraces all the neighbors. A study of these three McCarthys presents a demanding either/or for us, either self-serving calculation or the public good. It is an either/or that has nothing to do with party politics or with being liberal or conservative. Rather, it has to do with the kind of speech (and therefore the kind of public conduct and public policy) that will foster a viable covenantal, democratic society. Thus we can watch as Edgar Bergen moves his lips for Charlie; or we may ask who moved their lips for Joe's words, or who now moves the lips of Kevin's duplicity. We may be prompted by the questions of Joseph Welch concerning decency, the decency of neighborly respect that makes civil society possible.

It turns out that biblical faith has from the outset understood that speech that is *demagogic, duplicitous,* or *cynical* is toxic for shared human life. On the one hand, Israel's wisdom teachers, drawing on a long common legacy, see that such speech has no future:

> A false witness will not go unpunished,
> and a liar will not escape. (Prov 19:5)

> A false witness will not go unpunished,
> And a liar will perish. (Prov 19:9)

On the other hand, Moses is terse and uncompromising:

> You shall not bear false witness against your neighbor. (Exod 20:16; Deut 5:20)

This is a conviction sharpened in the Sermon on the Mount:

> Let your word be "Yes, Yes," or "No, No"; anything more than this comes from the evil one. (Matt 5:37)

Patrick Miller, in his wisdom, has seen the deep and wide import of the Sinai prohibition:

> With the commandment against false witness, the covenantal requirements for living with one's neighbor move from dominant concern for *actions* to an explicit focus on *words* and *speaking*. It would be a mistake, however, to see this movement as one from more serious matters to lesser concerns. Quite the contrary. The prohibition against bearing false witness is not so much a general rule against lying as it is a guard against the capacity of words and speaking to endanger one's neighbor in various ways, or indeed, to bring about violation of the commandments that precede this one. Telling the truth is thus a neighbor matter. It is a form of the love of neighbor and a significant aspect of upholding communal relations. Safeguarding the neighbor by safeguarding truth is an inevitable sequence to the protection of the neighbor's marriage, life, and property, for lying against a neighbor creates a domino effect undoing the other safeguards. Truth or consequences is indeed the choice in speaking about one's neighbor.[2]

The McCarthy options of *puppeteering, demagoguery, or opportunism* present an important challenge for truth-telling, a work upon which a viable common future surely depends. In the face of such options, those of us

---

2. Miller, *Ten Commandments*, 343.

entrusted with truth-telling may need to move beyond our usual caution and cowardice to be bold truth-tellers in the name of the *truth-telling, truth-performing., truth-requiring* God.

20

The Peaceful Transfer of Real Power

TRANSFIGURATION
2 KINGS 2:1–12

No doubt many preachers will eschew this enigmatic text and choose texts that give easier access. I hope, to the contrary, that preachers will linger over this text, because it teems with interpretive thickness. The narrative specificity of this text includes a number of components that defy our every explanation:

In v. 8 Elijah takes his mantle and strikes the water. The waters part and they crossed on dry land. The narrative offers no explanation for this act. It is easy enough, however, to see in this event an allusion to the exodus narrative wherein the waters parted and dry land appeared:

> The Lord drove the sea back by a strong east wind all night, and turned the sea into *dry land;* and the waters were divided. The Israelites went into the sea on *dry ground*, the waters forming a wall for them on their right and on their left. (Exod 14:21–22)

Elijah reiterates the liberating wonder of the exodus. With Moses the wonder required a strong east wind. For Elijah all that was needed was his mantle, a sure sign that his mantle was permeated with transformative power.

In v. 9, Elisha asks for "a double share of your spirit." He does not ask for God's spirit, but for the spirit (= power, authority) of Elijah. In our verses, there is no such gift of that spirit to Elisha. If, however, we peak over into vv. 13–15 and back to 1 Kgs 20:19–21, we can see that Elijah's mantle is a sign and embodiment of extraordinary power. Indeed, in 2:13–15, Elisha strikes the water with the mantle of Elijah, an act that echoes Elijah's own act in the preceding verses. Again the waters parted, and again they passed over on dry land. It is evident that power has been transferred (peaceably). Elisha is infused with the capacity of Elijah. He too can perform an exodus!

In v. 11, Elijah "ascended" accompanied by chariots of fire and horses of fire, inscrutable tools of divine capacity. They are tools to which Elisha will have access in his unequal struggle with the Syrian king (see 6:17). More important, however, is the disclosure that Elijah did not die. Instead he is wondrously "taken up" in the power of God. Along with Enoch (Gen 5:24), Elijah is the only character in the Old Testament who does not die. As a result, Elijah is kept alive by God and kept "in reserve" for a return in power to continue the emancipatory work of YHWH. On "Transfiguration Sunday" we have this text in the lectionary of Elijah being "transfigured" before Elisha into a larger-than-history character who has a continuing role to play in the imagined future of Israel.

The response of Elisha in v. 12 is often taken as a lament, that is, because he is disconcerted to have Elijah go away. And that may be the case; but it need not be so. It could perhaps be Elisha's full and final recognition of who Elijah is. He calls him "father" in an acknowledgement of his own "inheritance of power" as his "son" and successor. He also identifies Elijah as a powerful instrument for YHWH. This must have been an awesome moment for Elisha, for he recognizes both Elijah's inscrutable power and the fact that he is now the bearer of that power. This is a moment when Elisha becomes "woke" to his own vocation. In this utterance we see that Elisha is also "transfigured" into a role of prophetic power and responsibility.

The final action of this paragraph in v. 12 is peculiarly odd and inexplicable. Perhaps Elisha's tearing of his clothes is an act of grief work over the departure of Elijah. Or perhaps it is an act of desperation as he takes up his new role. Or perhaps the act is the dramatic rending of his "old self" to be dressed and equipped for his "new self" in his new role just bequeathed to him. This possibility could perhaps be an anticipation of the new "self" of which the author of Ephesians writes that is marked by "true righteousness and holiness" (Eph 4:23–24).

These four actions are stated tersely and without elaboration. The interpreter does not need to "explain." I suggest that these several elements in the story are signs that articulate and assure that what is happening in this narrative is not "ordinary." These are not ordinary characters and their lives are not ordinary lives. Rather, their lives are permeated with thick specificities that attest that God's transformative power is at work in and through them. Thus the interpretive point may be that human lives, some human lives, are laden with transformative power that is not amenable to our usual categories of explanation. This narrative thus invites us to wonder and anticipate concerning human persons laden with God's power. The narrative makes the claim that these particular human persons, Elijah and Elisha, are a continuation of the exodus tradition and are authorized to liberate and to permit the emergence of new life beyond all old bondages.

Once we have seen this pervasive interest in the narrative, I suggest we may identify *three lines of interpretation*. First, Elijah, taken up "into heaven" is held in abeyance by God for future deployment into the world. This means that wherever Elijah may yet emerge, history is open to new possibility. He did not die but has kept his awesome generative power for future enactment. This remarkable claim shows up variously in the ongoing tradition. In the Christian Old Testament (as distinct from the Hebrew Bible), the very last verses of the very last book in the Old Testament anticipate the return of Elijah who will perform reconciliation:

> Lo, I will send you the prophet Elijah before the great and terrible day of the Lord comes. He will turn the hearts of parents to their children and the hearts of children to their parents, so that I will not come and strike the land with a curse. (Mal 4:5–6)

Where Elijah is expected, history is not closed off in despair because he will bring newness. Thus the Christian Old Testament voices an openness to the newness that follows in the New Testament.

The New Testament makes a claim on this tradition of Elijah. At the outset, the gospel of Luke, through an angelic declaration, anticipates one with "the spirit and power of Elijah," a reference to John the Baptizer:

> With the spirit and power of Elijah he will go before him, to turn the hearts of parents to their children, and the disobedient to the wisdom of the righteous, to make ready a people prepared for the Lord. (Luke 1:17)

This one will perform reconciliation. In Luke 9:18–20, some identify Jesus with Elijah; this mention of him is just preceding the narrative of the transfiguration of Jesus in which Elijah also appears (9:30). This claim concerning Elijah exhibits the way in which the New Testament gospel is filled with expectation funded by the memory of Elijah. That expectation will not be contained in the categories of the ordinary. Something quite different is anticipated that is linked to the memory of Elijah.

Jews at Passover host a seat for the presence of Elijah, in anticipation that he will participate in the great meal of emancipation. For Jews and for Christians, Elijah is a cipher to declare that God's work in history through transformative human agents is not yet finished. We may expect yet more transformations to occur that are authorized by the Lord of all history, performed by human agents.

Second, Elisha by this narrative is unloosed into the narratives that follow.[1] Once Elisha is authorized and empowered, he occupies a series of narratives in which he overrides the circumstances of death (2 Kgs 4:32–37), leprosy (5:1–27), war (6:8–23), and famine (6:24—7:20). It is important to notice, moreover, that Elisha, an uncredentialed outsider, is able to transform (transfigure?) social reality. He does this, moreover, in the face of royal opposition while the various unnamed kings in the narrative are themselves unable to do any transformative work. In sum, the narratives of Elisha portray a human character capable of transformative action who lives outside the power structure of the monarchs. It surely cannot be accidental or incidental that in many ways the wonder stories of Jesus appear to replicate those of the Elisha narratives. Not unlike Elisha, Jesus is also an outsider who does the transformative work that established power cannot do.

Both Elijah and Elisha are carriers of historical possibility that refuses the shut-down of despair or the status quo of human *hubris*. Both of them keep the historical process open to possibility that runs well beyond the domesticated imagination of their contemporaries. In particular, they oppose and resist the royal power structure that has an ideological stake in closing off new historical possibility.

Third, Elijah and Elisha constitute not only a pair of wonder workers. They are linked as initiator and successor. Or we might say that our text witnesses to "prophetic succession" that is not unlike "apostolic succession." This dimension of their relationship is important because it alludes to the fact that wonder workers for justice in every generation are not isolated self-starters or individualized agents. Rather, they are heirs to a long tradition that continues to be lively and generative. Thus Elisha, as noted above,

---

1. See Brueggemann, *Testimony to Otherwise*.

receives "the spirit of Elijah," a force that equips him for his great risky transformative action.

Interpretation of this text may offer the good news that history is kept open by and for human actors who live in a "succession" of bold expectation that runs well beyond the status quo of despair and injustice. Our interpretation and articulation of good news in our present historical circumstance is exactly that history is kept open, open for new possibility by empowered human agents. This is particularly good news now, for it is easy enough, in the face of covid, economic shut-down, and the climate crisis, to settle for despair or, at best, for the most compelling status quo we can imagine. This narrative refuses that conventional settlement and insists on new possibility of a radical difference. That future is kept open to new possibility, moreover, only when and where and if there are human agents who carry the power to enact newness. These particular human agents will, every time, stand in a succession of those who refuse the closure of history to which ideology summons us. Imagine that it is the readers of this text who may be inundated with the future willed by God that may happen among us. The parting of the waters after the fashion of Moses, first by Elijah (2 Kgs 2:8) and then by Elisha (2 Kgs 2:14) attests that no Pharonic force can stop the life-giving newness of God when there are human agents infused with courage, freedom, and imagination, all gifts of the spirit. The narrative attests that power has been transferred from Elijah to Elisha. This is indeed real power, the kind that moves relentlessly beyond every status quo.

21

Traitor to Your Class

OUR GREAT ADVOCATE FOR environmental responsibility, Bill McKibben, has a wondrously rich suggestive phrasing in *Sojourners*.[1] The title of his opinion piece is "The Rich Shall Destroy the Earth." He observes that the climate crisis is caused by the self-indulgence of the 1%, a group in which he includes all who have an annual income of $109,000 or more! He observes that the climate crisis can get relief if:

> the richest people should strive to change their habits . . . the real hope is that some of those same people will actually involve themselves in the battle to change the political and economic structures that keep us burning fossil fuel.[2]

McKibben concludes, "We need, as it were, some *class betrayal*," in which some of the 1% act against the interest of their own perceived wellbeing and become engaged for the sake of the common good. (I remember that Franklin D. Roosevelt in my childhood, with his social programs, was labeled "a traitor to his class" because he acted contrary to the economic interest of the wealthy class to which he himself belonged.) McKibben's call is for just such a reversal of interest and investment.

In response to McKibben, I have reflected on "class betrayal" in the Bible. Let us begin with reference to the 1% in the Old Testament, a pyramid of wealth and power atop of which sat the Davidic King. It turns out,

---

1. McKibben, "The Rich Shall Destroy the Earth."
2. McKibben, "The Rich Shall Destroy the Earth," 17.

Lament That Generates Covenant

predictably, that the kings in Jerusalem were "takers," just as old Samuel had anticipated:

> He will *take* your sons and appoint them to his chariots and to be horsemen, and to run before his chariots; and he will appoint for himself commanders of thousands and commanders of fifties, and some to plow his ground and to reap his harvest, and to make his implements of war and the equipment of his chariots. He will *take* your daughters to be perfumers and cooks, and bakers. He will *take* the best of your fields and vineyards and olive orchards and give them to his courtiers. He will *take* one-tenth of your grain and of your vineyards and give it to his officers and his courtiers. He will *take* your male and female slaves, and the best of your cattle and donkeys, and put them to his work. He will *take* one-tenth of your flocks, and you shall be his slaves. (1 Sam 8:11–17)

The master "taker" in the memory of Israel is Solomon who amassed for himself a surplus of cheap labor (1 Kgs 5:13–16), silver and gold (10:14–25), wives and concubines (11:3), extravagant food for the day (4:22–23), plus an effective tax-collecting system (4:7–19). And his father David, before him, was surely a taker; we are told that he wanted Bathsheba and "he *took* her" (2 Sam 12:4). After David and Solomon, the royal dynasty continued its habit of "taking."

For that reason we are caught up short when we arrive, over 300 years later, at King Josiah (639–609 BCE). He inherited wealth and power from that long line of kings. But then we have this remarkable narrative concerning Josiah in which he was disturbed by the finding of a Torah scroll, a scroll most often taken to be some form of the book of Deuteronomy. It is reported that Josiah was stunned and staggered when he heard the commands and the sanctions of the scroll:

> When the king heard the words of the book of the law, he tore his clothes. Then the king commanded the priest Hilkiah, Ahikam son of Shaphan, Achbor son of Micaiah, Shaphan, the secretary, and the king's servant Asaiah, saying, "Go, inquire of the LORD for me, for the people, and for all Judah, concerning the words of the book that has been found; for great is the wrath of the LORD that is kindled against us, because our ancestors did not obey the words of the book, to do according to all that is written concerning us." (2 Kgs 22:11–13)

If as seems likely, this scroll is the book of Deuteronomy, then the king hears (likely for the first time) the mandates to social justice (see Deut

16:18) that concern sustenance for the most vulnerable—widows, orphans, and immigrants (see 24:17–22). Because of that dazzling reading from the old tradition, Josiah the king instituted a great religious, social reform that reconstituted Israel as a people of the covenant, that is, with covenantal obligations and covenantal promises (2 Kgs 23:1–3).

The narrative of King Josiah is indeed dramatic, as it must be. It is inescapably dramatic whenever someone of money and power becomes "woke" to social reality and acts in daring ways against the evident interest of that money and power. That is what Josiah did. He violated his social economic interest. He betrayed his social class. He chose an alternative way of governance that reached beyond the safe self-protective concerns of his 1%. His bold alternative action opened more historical possibility to his realm and especially to those who had been left out and left behind.

Of course, Josiah was a glaring exception in the royal timeline. He was succeeded by his son, Jehoiakim (609–598) after the brief interlude of Josiah's first son, Jehoahaz (609; see 2 Kgs 23:31–37). Jehoiakim did not share his father's social vision or social passion and returned to a royal "normal." He was not amenable to the demands of the Torah. As a consequence, he receives a standard negative verdict form the historian:

> He did what was evil in the sight of the LORD, just as all his ancestors had done. (2 Kgs 23:37)

Thus the father broke ranks and betrayed his class of privilege. By contrast his son was safely contained within the ideology of privilege.

The prophet Jeremiah offers a searing contrast between the royal father and his royal son. The prophet roundly condemns the son for his generic avarice:

> Woe to him who builds his house by unrighteousness,
>   and his upper rooms by injustice;
> who makes his neighbors work for nothing,
>   and does not give them their wages;
> who says, "I will build myself a spacious house with large upper rooms,"
>   and who cuts out windows for it,
> paneling it with cedar,
>   and painting it with vermilion.
> Are you a king because you compete in cedar? (Jer 22:13–15a)

The prophetic indictment includes a generic notion of "unrighteousness and injustice," and the double specificity of *exploitative labor* and *extravagant housing*. The rhetorical question of v. 15a is scathing denunciation; it accuses the king of thinking that having luxurious wood (cedar) permits and equates with the legitimacy of power and privilege.

Jeremiah believes that in a world governed by the God of covenant such self-indulgent exploitation leads to harsh consequences. Thus the "woe" of v. 13 is specified in vv. 18–19 by an anticipation of the scandalous death of the exploitative king:

> With the burial of a donkey he shall be buried—
>   dragged out and thrown out beyond the gates of Jerusalem. (v. 19)

In order to accent the deep failure of Jehoiakim as king, in the middle verses of this poem Jeremiah pauses to offer two verses concerning the royal father of Jehoiakim, Josiah:

> Did not your father eat and drink and do justice and righteousness?
>   Then it was well with him.
> He judged the cause of the poor and needy;
>   Then it was well.
> Is not this to know me?
> Says the LORD. (vv. 15b–16)

Josiah, says the prophet, practiced "justice and righteousness," an exact counter to the "unrighteousness and injustice" in v. 13. Josiah's path of "justice and righteousness" leads him to care for and engage on behalf of the "poor and needy." That is, the king, propelled by the Torah of Deuteronomy, mobilized royal power to assure economic viability for the disadvantaged, exactly what Deuteronomy requires. And then Jeremiah voices one of the most stunning verses in all of Scripture: "Is not this to know me?" The prophet equates *care for the poor and needy* with *knowledge of God*! This is how we know God! Knowledge of God is not speculative, abstract, propositional, or theoretical. It is a practice! It is the performance of neighborliness!

This remarkable utterance by Jeremiah provides a model of contrast:

- Jehoiakim reduces his life to control, privilege, entitlement, and extravagance. His is a normal "royal" life in ancient Israel.
- Josiah breaks with that ideology and devotes his royal power to the common good. He does indeed betray his royal class of takers. He does so at the behest of the ancient Torah requirement.

We may consider one other character in this royal drama in Jerusalem. After Babylon's first incursion into Jerusalem in 598 that the prophet took to be divine judgment (2 Kgs 24:10–17), Zedekiah was established as the next king (24:18–20). He was dealt a very bad hand as the city was devastated by the Babylonians (24:13–17). The narrative in the book of Jeremiah suggests that Zedekiah had an impulse, in the face of the destruction, to imitate his brother, Josiah, and govern according to neighborly Torah. Perhaps he understood that something radical had to be done in the face of the big challenges that the city faced. It is reported that the king took the most radical act of the Torah and released debt-slaves from their bondage; he cancelled their debts (Jer 34:8–10; see Deut 15:1–18). This royal act was a stunning betrayal of his class, for the 1% privilege and power lives by the management of debt that keeps "lesser people" in their dependent places. Zedekiah was prepared to commit this cancelation of debt and emancipate people from debt and bondage. This action is as astonishing as was that of his brother, Josiah. But then, abruptly, we are told:

> But afterward they turned around and took back the male and female slaves they had set free, and brought then again into subjection as slaves. (Jer 34:11)

Zedekiah had been *almost persuaded* to obey Torah, and then was not:

> "Almost persuaded" now to believe;
> "Almost persuaded" Christ to receive;
> Seems now some soul to say, "Go Spirit, go Thy way,
> Some more convenient day On Thee I'll call."
> "Almost persuaded," harvest is past!
> "Almost persuaded," doom comes at last
> "Almost" cannot avail;
> "Almost" is but to fail!
> Sad, sad, that bitter wail—
> "Almost" but lost.[3]

We are not told why the king reversed field. Maybe the king faced great pressure to the contrary from his "class." Maybe the economic loss by emancipation was more than he could bear. In any case, Zedekiah lacked the resolve and fortitude to see through the emancipation. He reneged, and in reneging he defied the Torah. He returned to the "normalcy" of the 1% that regards debt management as a proper preoccupation, and that does

---

3. Bliss, "Almost Persuaded."

not flinch from the bondage and suffering of those who could not pay their bills. Zedekiah had a chance to act like his brother Josiah. In the end, however, he opted for the exploitative ways of his nephew, Jehoiakim, ways that are conventional for his 1% companions.

It is not a surprise that this renege evokes a prophetic oracle (34:12–22). In the oracle the prophet bears witness to the Torah requirement (v. 14). He commends the king for his almost embrace of Torah obedience (v. 15). And then he indicts the king for "profaning my name" (v. 16). It is noteworthy that *exploitation of the poor through debt management* is equated with *profanation of God's holy name*. The equation calls to mind the Proverb:

> Those who mock the poor insult their Maker;
> those who are glad at calamity will not go unpunished. (Prov 17:5)

The prophet condemns the king for not "granting release" to "your neighbors and friends" (v. 17; the Hebrew has "brother and neighbor"). From that comes a torrent of danger to the king and his city. The profanation of God's name via the exploitation of the neighbor has consequences that even the royal 1% in Jerusalem will not escape.

While the books of Kings offers us the royal time-line and chronology, it is the prophetic book of Jeremiah that fills in the timeline with narrative specificity. In that narrative specificity, we see three royal characters of the 1% choosing different stances:

- *Josiah* chose, against his class, the way of neighborly Torah;
- *Jehoiakim* engages the self-serving ideology of his 1% to the disregard of the Torah;
- *Zedekiah* probes the possibility of Torah obedience like that of Josiah, but then opts, after the manner of Jehoiakim, for the "evil" of the 1%.

According to Jeremiah Zedekiah's royal choice led to disaster:

> I am going to command, says the LORD, and will bring them back [the Babylonians] to this city; and they will fight against it, and take it, and burn it with fire. The towns of Judah I will make a desolation without inhabitant. (Jer 34:22)

This consequence fills out with specificity the generic "woe" uttered over Jehoiakim (22:13). As the prophetic text has it, the royal 1% in old Jerusalem, with its self-indulgent, self-aggrandizing ideology, can imagine itself immune to the risks of history. Their ideological choice precludes attention to or investment in the common good that is essential to a viable future for the community.

Jeremiah presents Josiah as a "class betrayer." And now McKibben calls for more class betrayers. When I read McKibben I thought, "Yes, that is a good summons. I thought that and then I read that includes everyone with annual income of $109,000 is of the 1%. Imagine, I am a member of the 1%! And very likely, dear reader, you are as well.

Most of us in the 1% do not identify ourselves in that way. And because we do not, we easily imagine that the climate crisis belongs to others. But Bill tells us otherwise. It is a matter of *recognizing our class membership*; and the way in which we have over time inhaled a great deal of entitlement and privilege. And then it is a matter of *letting the social reality of the crisis into our awareness*. And then we are left with a future to some great extent in our own hands.

- It could be (after Josiah) a future of solidarity with the poor and needy, and so toward the rule of God that leads to a different life,
- Or it could be (after Jehoiakim) a continuing indifference that continues to do damage to creation, or
- Most likely for most of us, we are not unlike Zedekiah, almost persuaded.

We know what is to be done,
But it turns out to be too demanding.
McKibben echoes a quote from Pope Francis:

> In fact, the Earth must be taken care of, cultivated, and protected; we cannot continue to squeeze it like an orange. And we can say this, taking care of the Earth is a human right.[4]

It turns out that it is just like the Torah of Deuteronomy has said:

> I set before you today life and prosperity, death and adversity. (Deut 30:15)

Nothing life-giving turns out to be easy! McKibben ends with three "needs":

> We need, as it were, some class betrayal.
> Or, we need a renewed and powerful uprising of the people whose lives are most stunted and future most degraded.

---

4. McKibben, "The Rich Shall Destroy the Earth," 17.

Or, we need some strikingly successful attempt to build a sense of shared humanity, a real solidarity.[5]

Are you like me, "Almost persuaded"?

---

5. McKibben, "The Rich Shall Destroy the Earth," 17.

22

We Will Get Through This Together

It has become a familiar mantra among us: "We will get through this together." It is on the lips of many public officials including the president. It intends to reassure, to assuage our anxiety, and bring calm. There is, moreover, a self-serving element in the mantra with an implied addition, "Trust me." Trust me to get us through this together.

While such an assurance is welcome, it also makes one wonder: who is the "we" in this mantra?

- The "we" might include all those who have gotten the vaccine, including those who have jumped the line ahead of others. But it does not, surely, include the more than 550,000 dead from COVID-19. And for now it does not include their grieving families.

- The "we" might include all those who have received government assistance, including those who have gamed the system for a disproportionate share. But it does not, surely, include all those who have lost their jobs or their businesses due to a necessary shut-down.

- The "we" might include the advantaged children of the well-connected who have prospered with on-line schooling, who have benefitted from vigorous parental support, state of the art technology and, consequently, high motivation. But it does not, surely, include the many children who lack such privilege, such support, such technology, and such motivation.

It turns out, in my judgment, that the mantra is in part a denial; it disregards the victims of the virus, the victims of the economic slow-down, and the victims of on-line schooling. It is in part denial, but it is also in part an illusion because it is unmistakably clear that "we" will not all get through this together. Many of us surely will, but many of us just as surely will not.

When I consider how many of us are well and how many of us will get through this in good shape, my mind drifts to an odd verse in the prophet Amos:

> Thus says the LORD: As the shepherd rescues from the mouth of the lion *two legs, or a piece of an ear*, so shall the people of Israel who live in Samaria be rescued, with *the corner of a couch and part of a bed*. (Amos 3:12)

This verse is odd because it is prose in the midst of poetry, suggesting it is an intrusion. Nonetheless this verse, like much of Amos, concerns Samaria, the capital city of Northern Israel. We are familiar with the confrontation the prophet had with the priest at the royal shrine of Bethel (7:10–17). Amos was accused by the priest there of conspiracy; the charge against the prophet distorted his message in order to make the accusation of conspiracy stick (7:11). The priest seeks to silence the prophet and his unwelcome message of coming disaster. He avers that such negative talk is not permitted in the sphere of the king, certainly not in the sanctuary of the king:

> O seer, go flee away to the land of Judah, earn your bread there, and prophesy there; but never again prophesy at Bethel, for it is the king's sanctuary, and it is a temple of the kingdom. (7:12–13)

Amos, however, persists in his anticipation and in his utterance that big trouble is coming to Israel and to Samaria, whether or not the king wants to hear of it:

> Therefore, thus says the LORD:
> Your wife shall become a prostitute in the city,
>   and your sons and your daughters shall fall by the sword,
> and your land shall be parceled out by line,
>   you yourself shall die in an unclean land,
> and Israel shall surely go into exile away from its land. (7:17)

The prophet anticipates death in war, confiscation of the land, and exile away from the land. He anticipated the undoing of all that royal Samaria believed to be an assured given.

It turned out, in fact, that the anticipation of the prophet was vindicated. In 722 BCE the army of Sargon, the Assyrian, came and routed the city, and deported leading citizens:

> Then the king of Assyria invaded all the land and came to Samaria; for three years he besieged it. In the ninth year of Hoshea the king of Assyria captured Samaria; he carried the Israelites away to Assyria. He placed them in Halah, on the Habor, the river of Gozan, and in the cities of the Medes. (2 Kgs 17:5–6)

The vigorous royal-priestly stonewalling in Samaria and Bethel did not alter and could not retard historical reality that the prophet took as evidence of God's governance of history.

What interests me in this odd verse (Amos 3:12) is that Amos responds to the official line that "We will get through this together." We will get through the threat to Samaria together; Amos answers the illusionary assurance of the priest via the image of a shepherd and a sheep. Let Assyria be the lion; let Samaria be the vulnerable sheep. The shepherd seeks to rescue the sheep by pulling it out of the mouth of the lion. But all that he can pull out and rescue is "two legs" of the sheep and "a piece of an ear" of the sheep. That is all that is rescued! So says the prophet, it will be like that: Samaria will be saved from the Assyrians. But all that will be rescued will be "the corner of a couch" or "the part of a bed;" otherwise all will be lost in the same way that the rest of the sheep will be lost to the lion. (Indeed archaeologists claim to have found a piece of an ivory bed in the ruins of the city, a sign of extreme luxury; see Amos 6:4.) But that is all. The notion that Samaria will be rescued from Assyria is an illusion. Or it is a denial that the capitol city will be destroyed by a force dispatched by YHWH. In prophetic horizon, the "we" that will get through this is a wee remnant, only two legs and the piece of an ear, the corner of a couch or part of a bed, nothing more.

The prophet speaks in imagery. The point is not a literal one. The point, rather, is to recognize that the cost of a disordered public life is inescapably very great. The savage cost cannot be denied or understated. Most of the sheep is lost; most of the house (palace) is done in. The priest in Bethel is lying when he says, "We will get through this together." Because many sheep, many houses, many cities, many people will not "get through."

Good liberal that I am, I am eager that President Biden's American Rescue Plan Act should succeed. But we should not be under any illusion. We should not engage in any denial. The truth is that the "we" that we will get through this together consists in those of us who are privileged and connected and, well, lucky. The "we" that survives in wellbeing is limited and not comprehensive. It is important that this truth be told, acknowledged, and performed, even if the official mantra says otherwise.

It is surely the work of the faith community to be truth-tellers about those who have dropped out of the successful, rescued "we." It is important that this other "we" of loss be remembered and taken with great seriousness. That of course is what Amos did. He engaged in lament for the loss that the priest wanted to deny:

> Hear this word that I take up over you in lamentation, O house of Israel:
> Fallen no more to rise,
> is maiden Israel;
> Forsaken her land,
> with no one to raise her up. (5:1–2)

The prophet engaged in petition for his community in its helpless vulnerability:

> O Lord GOD, forgive, I beg you!
> How can Jacob stand?
> He is so small. (7:2)

> O Lord GOD, cease, I beg you!
> How can Jacob stand?
> He is so small! (7:5)

Eventually the prophet would engage in recovery and restoration; but not too soon.

So imagine the church as a venue of grieving and petition:

- *naming* the lost, one by one, as long as is required;
- *advocating* for those who have lost jobs and businesses;
- *lobbying* for the "left behind" children who have not had the benefit of privilege, advantage, and technology in their families.

Unless we do that with some sustained intentionality—*naming*, *advocating*, and *lobbying*—we who "get through this together" will not long grieve or remember. We will not reallocate funds. We will, as soon as we can, return to the old "normal" that disregards the dead, forgets the lost, and neglects the left behind. The church in its remembering must, I suggest, contradict the ubiquitous mantra, "We will get through this together." Because many of us will not. While we get through this together, Amos holds up for us two legs and the piece of an ear. While we watch Amos's poignant reminder to us, we might remember as well that later trope on a shepherd:

> Which of you, having a hundred sheep and losing one of them, does not leave the ninety-nine in the wilderness and go after the one that is lost until he finds it? (Luke 15:4)

Eventually Amos will end in hope:

> On that day I will raise up
> the booth of David that is fallen,
> and repair its breaches,
> and raise up its ruins,
> and rebuild it as in the days of old. (Amos 9:11)

But not too soon. Before he does that, Amos will be in anticipation of the later imagery of Ezekiel:

> I myself will be the shepherd of my sheep, and will make them lie down, says the Lord God. I will seek the lost, and I will bring back the strayed, and I will bind up the injured, and I will strengthen the weak, but the fat and the strong I will destroy. I will feed them with justice. (Ezek 34:15–16)

Not too much credence should be given to "the fat and the strong" who will want to move on quickly to the old normalcy. The church lingers; it does not flinch at loss. It engages in no cover up or false assurances. It grieves. It prays. Belatedly it remembers promises and sets about to keep them.

23

When the Music Starts Again

ANY FAMILY OR COMMUNAL festive occasion can become a "sign" or a marker. It could be a graduation, a birthday, a funeral, or a reunion. But let us consider a wedding . . . a wedding as a "sign" or a marker of social, historical significance. This is how it was for the ancient prophet Jeremiah as he watched his beloved Jerusalem sink into misery. He must have thought, "Let us consider a wedding as a significant social, historical marker and sign." As he thought that, he noticed that weddings in the city had stopped. There were no more weddings in Jerusalem! He took the cessation of weddings to be, on the one hand, a sign of *God's active sovereignty*, and on the other hand, *a measure of the dislocation* that the city must face in time to come.

JEREMIAH 7

The book of Jeremiah has the prophet comment on the matter of weddings three times (though it could be that the three citations are editorial reiteration). At the end of his "temple sermon" (Jeremiah 7) in which he anticipates the gruesome sight of many dead bodies piled up (7:32–33), Jeremiah concludes:

> And I will bring an end to the sound of mirth and gladness, the voice of the bride and bridegroom in the cities of Judah and in the streets of Jerusalem; for the land shall become a waste. (7:34)

There will be no singing, or dancing, no laughter, no celebration. All weddings will be ended, a sign that the city will end in "waste." In that "sermon," it is anticipated that the end of weddings comes about, according to the prophet, because of a systemic violation of Torah, a contradiction of the purpose of God:

> Will you steal, murder, commit adultery, swear falsely, make offerings to Baal, and go after other gods that you have not known, and then come and stand before me in this house . . . ? (vv. 9–10a)

The shame of such violation is compounded by the fact that after such systemic violation, the perpetrators come piously to the temple and imagine that they are "safe and secure from all alarms," hiding like a "den of robbers" (vv. 10–11).

JEREMIAH 16

The point is a second time articulated in Jeremiah 16. In that prose passage the prophet anticipates a wholesale devastation of the city. God declares:

> Do not enter the house of mourning, or go to lament or bemoan them; for I have taken away my *peace* from this people, says the LORD, my *steadfast love* and *mercy*. Both great and small shall die in this land. (vv. 5–6)

The city cannot and will not prosper without the divine gift of peace, steadfast love, and mercy. After a devastating portrayal of massive death, the cessation of weddings is a measure of the trouble to come:

> I am going to ban from this place, in your days and before your eyes, the voice of mirth and the voice of gladness, the voice of the bridegroom and the voice of the bride. (v. 9)

In response to this verdict, the prophet has his people wonder why such trouble has come upon their city:

> They will say to you, "Why has the LORD pronounced all this great evil against us? What is our iniquity? What is the sin that we have committed against the LORD our God"? (v. 10)

And the prophetic response is:

> It is because your ancestors have forsaken me, says the LORD, and have gone after other gods and have served and worshipped them,

and have forsaken me and have not kept my law; and because you have behaved worse than your ancestors, for here you are, every one of you, following your stubborn evil will, refusing to listen to me. (vv. 11–12)

JEREMIAH 25

The theme is reiterated a third time in Jeremiah 25. In this version the point is made more specific with reference to the coming of the Babylonian army of Nebuchadnezzar who will utterly destroy the city and reduce it to shame and humiliation. The prohibition of weddings is linked to a climactic assertion of ruin and waste at the hand of the Babylonians:

> I am going to send all of the tribes of the north, says the LORD, even King Nebuchadnezzar of Babylon, my servant, and I will bring them against this land and its inhabitants, and against all the nations around; I will utterly destroy them, and make them an object of horror and hissing, and an everlasting disgrace. And I will banish from them the sound of mirth and the sound of gladness, the voice of the bridegroom and the voice of the bride, the sound of the millstones and the light of the lamp. This whole land shall become a ruin and a waste, and these nations shall serve the king of Babylon seventy years. (vv. 9–11)

It will be evident that this prophetic tirade does not hesitate or blink at the direct linkage between *historical eventuality* and *divine governance*. In all three usages, the cause of cessation of weddings is divine agency:

- I will bring an end. (7:34)
- I am going to banish. (16:9)
- I will banish. (25:10)

I call attention to this because this is a direct linkage that most of us would not make and almost none of us would want to make. We do not readily imagine God's governance to be so direct; nor do we consider that the God of covenant would so willfully cause the suffering and death of God's own people.[1] It is nonetheless important for us to notice (and perhaps flinch) that the prophetic tradition has no such caution in making that direct claim for governance. This lack of reticence on the part of the tradition

---

1. The reader may notice that in my little book, Brueggemann, *Virus as Summons to Faith*, I have given careful nuance to this difficult matter.

may give us some nerve and courage to imagine what it is like to live in a world where the purposes of God cannot be mocked with impunity. In the end God will not be mocked, not by our wealth, not by our wisdom, and not by our power. The weddings stopped. The music was silenced. The laughter ceased. Historical circumstance was too sobering. Social reality was too devastating. The songs stuck in our throats. Our feet were unmoving on the floor. Maybe there were weddings, but no glad sounds. Or maybe not at all, because lived reality had sunk deeply into an unmanageable pause.

Such poetic extremity as these verses of Jeremiah might give us an angle of vision on our social "shut down" amid the pandemic. Among us it is as though the celebration has stopped, that singing has silenced and the dancing paralyzed. Weddings delayed, family reunions postponed, churches vacated, schools hit and miss on-line and in person, and cinemas darkened, sports events without fans. Social life, social interaction, and social possibility all have come to a halt (except for some daring super-spreaders!) The pandemic is reason enough as an explanation for the silencing shut down. We do not need to look further for an explanation. The prophetic tradition, daring otherwise, pushes back further to the sovereignty of God who occupies active verbs like "banish" and "bring to an end." We would not push that far for an explanation; the silencing, nonetheless, is a stunning reminder of how unmistakably penultimate we are in managing the mysterious givens of our common life. Such an awareness of our penultimacy at least lets us resonate with the texts of Jeremiah. As we study the rising numbers of "cases" and "deaths" daily among us, we can draw close to the imagery of Jer 7:32–33 of corpses piled up for bird food; in our case, refrigerated trucks outside hospitals with many beloved bodies therein. As we stay safe in self-quarantine, we can weave into the urgency of Jer 16:7–8 with no "cup of consolation" to drink and the avoidance of "the house of feasting." As we notice that our number of cases and deaths is even worse than that of Brazil, we can expect that the United States is something of an object of "horror and hissing" among the nations (see Jer 25:9). And if Donald Trump would have his way, he would readily cast "China" in the role of Babylon who will "lay waste the whole land" (Jer 25:9–11).

Of course this is all an over-reading of Jeremiah. It nonetheless gives us pause as we read the old text that we claim to be "revelatory." What is "revealed" is that in and through the pandemic via this poetry is the truth that the world operates on a scale, at a pace, and in a texture other than one of our choosing. It is the singular work of poets, ancient and contemporary, to summon us into this mystery that is beyond our explanation or management. We begin with the obvious: the cessation of weddings. From that we work deeply into the mystery of our helplessness and our extensive efforts to "stay safe."

After these three instances of silenced weddings in Jeremiah, it may surprise and amaze us in a most welcome way that the prophet offers, eventually, a fourth usage of the imagery of a wedding in Jeremiah 33. That usage occurs in a chapter that is filled with the restorative promises of God. In vv. 1–9 we are offered a sweeping promise of recovery, healing, prosperity, security, and cleansing:

> I am going to bring it recovery and healing; I will heal them and reveal to them abundance of prosperity and security. I will restore the fortunes of Judah and the fortunes of Israel, and rebuild them as they were at first. I will cleanse them from all their guilt of their sin against me, and I will forgive all the guilt of their sin and rebellion against me. (vv. 6–7)

In vv. 12–13 we get a vision of a restored environment with viable agriculture in every part of the land:

> In the towns of the hill country, of the Shephelah, and of the Negev, in the land of Benjamin, the places around Jerusalem, and in the towns of Judah, flocks shall again pass under the hand of the one who counts them, says the LORD. (v. 13)

In vv. 14–22 it is promised that the Davidic line will be continued and restored, as certain as is God's covenant with day and night:

> If any of you could break my covenant with the day and my covenant with the night, so that day and night would not come at their appointed time, only then could my covenant with my servant David be broken, so that he would not have a son to reign on his throne. (vv. 20–21)

The chapter concludes with reassurance about God's most elemental promise, the one made to the offspring of Abraham:

> Only if I had not established my covenant with day and night and the ordinances of heaven and earth, would I reject the offspring of Jacob and my servant David and not choose any of his descendants as rulers over the offspring of Abraham, Isaac, and Jacob. For I will restore their fortunes, and will have mercy on them. (vv. 25–26)

This chapter mentions every possible dimension of God's commitment to Israel. It affirms that God is the keeper of every such promise.

And right in the midst of this overwhelming collage of promises is our theme:

> There shall once more be heard the voice of mirth and the voice of gladness, the voice of the bridegroom and the voice of the bride, the voices of those who sing, as they bring thank offerings to the house of the LORD. (33:11a)

Weddings will begin again! Life will be resumed in all its joy. Churches will be opened. Sports will be on offer. Cinemas will be available. Social life and social possibility are at hand!

In response to this renewal and restoration grounded in God's goodness, Israel will bring thank offerings. These offerings consist in generous material returns to the God of all goodness. And like all good thank offerings, these offerings are accompanied by words of acknowledgment, explaining why the generous gratitude of Israel:

> Give thanks to the LORD of hosts,
> for the LORD is good,
> for his steadfast love endures forever. (v. 11b)

For a time God's steadfast love had been absent in Israel (see 16:5). But not now! In the liturgic tradition of Israel, thank offerings are a glad recognition that God is good. Beyond that, God's abiding tenacious fidelity has persisted in and through the trouble, that is, in and through the pandemic. And then, as if to seal the deal, the text in v. 11 adds the great tag-word of rehabilitation: "Restore the fortunes." The promise is for return to something like normal, the measure of which is the singing, dancing, and laughter of wedding joy that every time is bet upon the future. It is no wonder that Jesus, in the wake of Jeremiah, appeals to the same imagery of wedding, bride, and bridegroom for the arrival of God's new future (Matt 25:1–13).

These four uses of the imagery of a wedding in Jeremiah—three negative and one positive—provide a screen through which to reread and reimagine our own pandemic with its *shut-down* and its *awaited reopening*. Beyond that, the imagery takes up this most treasured social practice of a wedding and lets it be a vehicle for articulation of God's steadfast love. The *silence and restoration* of wedding singing and dancing bespeak a regular feature of Israel's covenant faith, a faith practiced in *exile and homecoming*, a faith that in Christian parlance is reflected in *the shut-down of Good Friday* and *the opening of new life on Easter*. Judaism, and we Christians in its wake, can gladly attest:

> Weeping may linger for the night,
>   but joy comes in the morning. (Ps 30:5b)

The first two lines of this verse are awkward for us, because we do not readily speak of God's anger. But the Psalmist will give it voice:

> For his anger is for a moment;
>   his favor is for a lifetime. (Ps 30:5a)

The accent is on God's favor . . . for a lifetime, a very long time! There is, however, no denying the intense alienation from us that God knows. This is very hard to voice; we nonetheless observe it enacted in our empty social calendars.

Bibliography

Anonymous. "Fairest Lord Jesus." In *The United Methodist Hymnal*, 189. Nashville: United Methodist Publishing House, 1989.
Arana, Marie. *Silver, Sword & Stone: Three Crucibles in the Latin American Story*. New York: Simon & Schuster, 2019.
Barth, Karl. *Church Dogmatics* III/3: *The Doctrine of Creation*. Edited by G. W. Bromiley and T. F. Torrance. Translated by G. W. Bromiley and R. J. Ehrlich. Edinburgh: T. & T. Clark, 1960.
———. *Church Dogmatics*. IV/3, second half: *The Doctrine of Reconciliation*. Edited by G. W. Bromiley and T. F. Torrance. Translated by G. W. Bromiley. Edinburgh: T. & T. Clark, 1962.
Beck, Richard. *Unclean: Meditations on Purity, Hospitality, and Mortality*. Eugene, OR: Cascade Books, 2011.
Biéler, André. *Calvin's Economic and Social Thought*. Geneva: World Alliance of Reformed Churches, 2005.
Bliss, Philip P. "Almost Persuaded." (1871). In *Glory to God: Hymns, Psalms, & Spiritual Songs*. Louisville: Presbyterian Publishing, 2013.
Blyth, Mark. *Austerity: The History of a Dangerous Idea*. Oxford: Oxford University Press, 2013.
Boring, M. Eugene. *The Gospel of Matthew*. In *New Interpreter's Bible*. Vol. 8. Edited by Leander E. Keck. Nashville: Abingdon, 2015.
Brown, William P. *The Seven Pillars of Creation: The Bible, Science, and the Ecology of Wonder*. New York: Oxford University Press, 2010.
———. *Wisdom's Wonder: Character, Creation and Crisis in the Bible's Wisdom Literature*. Grand Rapids: Eerdmans, 2014.
Brueggemann, Walter. *Chosen? Reading the Bible amid the Israeli–Palestinian Conflict*. Louisville: Westminster John Knox, 2015.
———. *Testimony to Otherwise: The Witness of Elijah and Elisha*. St. Louis: Chalice, 2001.
———. *Virus as Summons to Faith: Biblical Reflections in a Time of Loss, Grief, and Uncertainty*. Eugene, OR: Cascade Books, 2020.
Claudius, Matthias. "We Plough the Fields, and Scatter." (1782). Translated by Jane M. Campbell (1861). In *The Presbyterian Hymnal*, 560. Louisville: Presbyterian Publishing, 1992.
Eagleton, Terry. *Reason, Faith, and Revolution: Reflections on the God Debate*. New Haven: Yale University Press, 2009.

Bibliography

The Evangelical Catechism: A New Translation for the 21st Century. Translated by Frederick R. Trost. Cleveland: Pilgrim, 2009.

Forché, Carolyn. *In the Lateness of the World*. New York: Penguin, 2020.

———. *What You Have Heard Is True: A Memoir of Witness and Resistance*. New York: Penguin, 2019.

Foroohar, Rana. *Makers and Takers: The Rise of Finance and the Fall of American Business*. New York: Crown Business, 2016.

Glantz, Aaron. *Homewreckers: How a Gang of Wall Street Kingpins, Hedge Fund Magnates Crooked Banks, and Vulture Capitalists Suckered Millions Out of Their Homes and Demolished the American Dream*. New York: Custom House, 2019.

Glory to God. Louisville: Westminster John Knox, 2013.

Goodrich, Frances et al. screenwriters. *It's a Wonderful Life*. Directed by Frank Capra. Liberty Films / RKO Radio Pictures, 1946.

Hartman, Saidiya V. *Scenes of Subjection: Terror, Slavery, and Self-Making in Nineteenth-Century America*. Race and American Culture. New York: Oxford University Press, 1997.

Hays, Richard B. *The Letter to the Galatians*. In *New Interpreter's Bible*, edited by Leander E. Keck, vol. 11. Nashville: Abingdon, 2000.

Joseph, Jane M. "On This Day Earth Shall Ring." (1924) In *The United Methodist Hymnal*, 248. Nashville: United Methodist Publishing House, 1989.

Kaiser, Walter. *The Book of Leviticus*. In *New Interpreter's Bible*. Vol. 1. Nashville: Abingdon, 1994.

Kelton, Stephanie. *The Deficit Myth: Modern Monetary Theory and the Birth of the People's Economy*. New York: PublicAffairs, 2020.

Lane, Nathan C. *The Compassionate but Punishing God: A Canonical Analysis of Exodus 34:6–7*. Eugene, OR: Pickwick Publications, 2010.

Lindberg, Carter, and Paul Wee, eds. *The Forgotten Luther: Reclaiming the Social-Economic Dimension of the Reformation*. Minneapolis: Lutheran University Press, 2016.

Martin, Civilla Durfee. "God Will Take Care of You." (1904). In *The United Methodist Hymnal*, 130. Nashville: United Methodist Publishing House, 1989.

McGann, Mary. *The Meal that Reconnects: Eucharistic Eating and the Global Food Crisis*. Collegeville, MN: Liturgical, 2020.

McGhee, Heather. *The Sum of Us: What Racism Costs Everyone and How We Can Prosper Together*. New York: One World, 2021.

McKibben, Bill. "The Rich Shall Destroy the Earth." *Sojourners*, March 2021, 16–17.

Meeks, M. Douglas. *God the Economist: The Doctrine of God and Political Economy*. Minneapolis: Fortress, 1989.

Miller, Patrick D. *The Ten Commandments*. Interpretation. Louisville: Westminster John Knox, 2009.

Neale, John Mason, trans. "Good Christian Friends, Rejoice." (1853) In *The United Methodist Hymnal*, 224. Nashville: United Methodist Publishing House, 1989.

Otto, Rudolf. *The Idea of the Holy: An Inquiry into the Non-rational Factor in the Idea of the Divine and Its Relation to the Rational*. 2nd ed. Translated by John W. Harvey. London: Oxford University Press, 1950.

Paton, Alan. "Meditation for a Young Boy Confirmed." *Christian Century*, October 13, 1954, 1238.

Pichichero, Christy. "Meghan and Harry Experienced Discriminatory Gaslighting: Here's How You Can Tell." NBC.com. Mar. 28, 2021. https://www.nbcnews.com/think/

opinion/meghan-harry-experienced-discriminatory-gaslighting-here-s-how-you-can-ncna1262235.
Sandel, Michael. *The Tyranny of Merit: What's Become of the Common Good?* New York: Farrar, Straus & Giroux, 2020.
Schafer, Roy. *Retelling a Life: Narration and Dialogue in Psychoanalysis.* New York: Basic Books, 1992.
Schui, Florian. *Austerity: The Great Failure.* New Haven: Yale University Press, 2014.
Scott, James C. *Domination and the Arts of Resistance: Hidden Transcripts.* New Haven: Yale University Press, 2008.
———. *Weapons of the Weak: Everyday Forms of Peasant Resistance.* New Haven: Yale University Press, 1985.
Souder, William. *Mad at the World: A Life of John Steinbeck.* New York: Norton, 2020.
Steinbeck, John. *The Grapes of Wrath.* New York: Modern Library, 1939.
Tankersley, Jim, and Jeanna Smialek. "Inflation Fears Fall by the Wayside in the Biden Era." *The New York Times*, Feb. 16, 2021, A1, A13.
Tennyson, Alfred. "In Memoriam A. H. H. OBIIT MDCCCXXXIII." 1833.
Tennyson, Alfred (lyrics), and George J. Elvey (music). "Strong Son of God, Immortal Love." 1862.
Trost, Frederick R., trans. *The Evangelical Catechism: A New Translation for the 21st Century.* Cleveland: Pilgrim, 2009.
Tull, Patricia K. *Isaiah 1–39.* Smyth & Helwys Bible Commentary. Macon, GA: Smyth & Helwys, 2010.
The United Methodist Hymnal. Nashville: United Methodist Publishing House, 1989.
Watts, Isaac. "Joy to the World." (1719) In *The United Methodist Hymnal*, 246. Nashville: United Methodist Publishing House, 1989.
Wesley, Charles. "Christ the Lord Is Risen Today." (1739) In *The United Methodist Hymnal*, 302. Nashville: United Methodist Publishing House, 1989.
Westermann, Claus. *The Psalms: Structure, Content & Message.* Translated by Ralph D. Gehrke. Minneapolis: Augsburg, 1980.
Young, Michael. *The Rise of Meritocracy.* 2nd ed. Classics in Organization and Management Series. London: Routledge, 1994.
Zakaria, Fareed. *Ten Lessons for a Post-Pandemic World.* New York: Norton, 2020.

Names Index

Arana, Marie, 97–98, 103

Barth, Karl, 42–43, 54–55
Beck, Richard, 34
Bergen, Edgar, 113, 116–17
Biéler, André, 7
Bliss, Philip P., 129
Blyth, Mark, 10
Boehner, John, 115
Boring, M. Eugene, 39
Brown, Mary, viii
Brown, William P., 8
Brueggemann, Tia, viii, 18
Brueggemann, Walter, 102, 123, 140

Claudius, Matthias, 59

Eagleton, Terry, 36
Elvey, George J., 48
Evans, Dale, 113

Fields, W. C., 113
Forché, Carolyn, 72–74, 104, 111
Foroohar, Rana, 19, 22

Glantz, Aaron, 19
Gómez Vides, Leonel, 72, 104
Goodrich, Frances, 13

Hartman, Saidiya V., 17–18
Hays, Richard B., 102

Johnson, Lyndon B., 108, 113
Joseph, Jane M., 64

Kaiser, Walter, 21–22
Kelton, Stephanie, 10–14
Kennedy, John F., 107–8

Lane, Nathan C., 41
Leo XIII, Pope, 7
Lindberg, Carter, 7
Lippert, Jane, 73–74, 77
Locke, John, 96

Martin, Civilla Durfee, 56
McCarthy, Charlie, 113–14, 116
McCarthy, Eugene, 113
McCarthy, Joe, 114–16
McCarthy, Kevin, 113, 115–16
McGann, Mary, 102
McGhee, Heather, 18–19, 22
McKibben, Bill, 125, 131–32
Meeks, M. Douglas, 7–8
Miller, Patrick D., 118

Neale, John Mason, 64

Otto, Rudolf, 21

Paton, Alan, 52
Pichichero, Christy, 29

Romero, Archbishop Óscar, 74, 77
Roosevelt, Franklin D., 125
Ryan, Paul, 115

Sandel, Michael, 57–59
Schafer, Roy, 49
Schui, Florian, 10

Names Index

Scott, James C., 17, 31
Sicknick, Brian, 107–8
Smialek, Jeanna, 7
Smith, Adam, 96
Smith, Margaret Chase, 114
Snerd, Mortimer, 114
Souder, William, 1
Steinbeck, John, 1–3, 5–6

Tankersley, Jim, 7
Tennyson, Alfred, 48–50
Trost, Frederick R., 4
Trump, Donald J., 11, 19, 23, 58, 115–16, 141

Tull, Patricia K., 116

Watts, Isaac, 23–25, 65
Wee, Paul, 7
Welch, Joseph, 115, 117
Wesley, Charles, 65
West, Mae, 113
Westermann, Claus, 70
Winfrey, Oprah, 29

Young, Michael, 56

Zakaria, Fareed, 39–40, 42, 44

Scripture Index

OLD TESTAMENT

Genesis
5:24	121
8:22	86
22	55
22:14	55
43:42	33–34

Exodus
2:23–24	105
3:7–9	106
5:8	30
5:17	30
8:20	17
10:3	17
10:7	17
12:48–49	99
12:49	99
14:21–22	120
15:21	105
16	9
16:3	9
19:5	76
19:6	42
20:16	118
24–25	106

Leviticus
	21
19:9–10	21
19:17–18	21
19:18	99
19:33–34	99
25:32	17
25:39–46	15
25:42	15–20

Numbers
14:18	41

Deuteronomy
	126, 128
5:1–18	94
5:20	118
7:6	76
14:2	76
15	16, 94
15:1–18	16, 93, 129
15:2–3	93
15:2	93
15:3	93
15:4	16, 94
15:7	93
15:9	93
15:11–12	96
15:11	16, 93
15:12	93
16:18	127
24:17–22	127
26:18	76
30:15	131
30:20	3
33:26	63

Scripture Index

Joshua
24:14–15 — 3

Judges
— 79, 81
1 — 98
3:7–11 — 79

1 Samuel
8:11–17 — 126
31:2 — 107

2 Samuel
1:19–27 — 107
1:23 — 107
1:26 — 107
2:14 — 107
12:4 — 126

1 Kings
4:7–19 — 126
4:22–23 — 126
5:13–16 — 126
10:14–25 — 126
11:3 — 126
20:19–21 — 121

2 Kings
2:1–12 — 120
2:8 — 120, 124
2:9 — 120
2:11 — 121
2:12 — 121
2:13–15 — 120
2:14 — 124
2:23–25 — 31
2:24 — 31
6:8–23 — 9
17:5–6 — 135
22:11–13 — 126
23:1–3 — 127
23:31–37 — 127
23:37 — 127
24–25 — 81

24:10–17 — 129
24:13–17 — 129
24:18–20 — 129

Nehemiah
9:6–37 — 37
9:11 — 33
9:32 — 37
9:36–37 — 37
10:31 — 38
10:32–39 — 38

Job
37:1 — 88
37:3–6 — 88
37:13 — 89
37:22–23 — 87
37:24 — 88
38 — 10, 90
38:4–37 — 87
38:4 — 87
38:11 — 87
38:25–30 — 54

Psalms
14:1 — 25
23 — 108
29 — 62–66
29:1–2 — 62
29:3–9a — 63
29:3 — 63
29:9b — 63
29:10–11 — 63
29:10 — 63
30 — 70
30:5a — 144
30:5b — 144
58 — 109
58:1–2 — 111
58:1 — 111
58:4 — 109
58:6 — 111
58:7–8 — 111
58:10–11 — 111
68:4 — 63

Scripture Index

73	24	107:28b–29	69
73:2–3	24	107:30b	69
73:17	24	107:31	69
73:18–20	24	107:32	70
73:19	24	107:41	71
73:23–26	28	107:43	71
86:15	41	136:10–15	30
89:3–4	81	145:15–16	8
89:33–37	81	147:1–6	89
90	24	147:1	89
90:1–6	25	147:4–9	8–9
90:7–9	25	147:7–11	89
90:10	25	147:13–14a	89
90:13	27	147:14b–18	89
90:13b–15	27	147:16–18	9
90:16	28	147:19–20	89
90:17	27	148:5–10	90
100	108–9	148:7–11	63
100:3	108	148:11	90
100:5	109		
103:3–5	51–52	**Proverbs**	
103:8	41	17:5	130
104:3	63	19:5	118
104:27–28	8	19:9	118
107	67	25:2	88
107:1–3	67		
107:2	70	**Ecclesiastes**	
107:4–9	68	9:1–3	25
107:5	68		
107:6	68	**Isaiah**	
107:6b–7	69	1:21–26	79
107:8	69	1:21–23	79
107:10–16	68	1:21	80
107:10	68	1:24–25	79
107:13	68	1:26	79
107:13b–14	69	1:26a	79
107:15	69	1:26b	79
107:17–22	68	5:8–10	59
107:17	68	6:8	26
107:19	68	6:9–13	26
107:19b–20	69	11:6–8	100
107:21	69	40–55	85
107:22	69, 70	40:8	85
107:22a	70	40:9	86
107:23–32	68	41:9–10	86
107:23–27	68		
107:25	68		

5

Isaiah (continued)

43:1–7	86
44:24–28	86
46:1–2	86
47:1–15	86
47:5–7	86
52:7	86
55	86
55:1	12
55:10–11	86, 90
55:10	86
55:11	86

Jeremiah

3:7	80
3:8	80
7:9–10a	139
7:10–11	139
7:32–33	138, 141
7:34	138, 140
16	139–40
16:5–6	139
16:5	143
16:7–8	141
16:9	139, 140
16:10	139
16:11–12	139–40
22:13–15a	127
22:13	130
22:15a	128
22:15b–16	128
22:18–19	128
22:19	128
23:5–6	81
25:9–11	141
25:9	141
25:10	140
33	80, 142
33:1–9	142
33:6–7	142
33:7	81
33:11a	143
33:11b	143
33:12–13	80, 142
33:13	142
33:14–22	142

33:14–16	81
33:19–22	81
33:20–21	142
33:25–26	142
34:8–10	129
34:11	129
34:12–22	130
34:13	142
34:14	130
34:15	130
34:16	130
34:17	130
34:22	130
38:4	32

Lamentations

3:22–23	41

Ezekiel

34	108
34:15–16	83
34:16	109
36:29–30	12

Daniel

12:1–4	76

Hosea

2	41, 42, 44
2:19–20	41
9:7	32

Amos

1:9	92
3:12	134, 135
5:1–2	136
6:4	135
7:2	136
7:5	136
7:10–17	134
7:11	134
7:12–13	134
7:17	134
9:11	134, 137

SCRIPTURE INDEX

9:13–14	83
9:13	12

Jonah
4:2	41

Micah
4:4	12

Nahum
1:3	63

Habakkuk
3:17–18	83

Malachi
3:16–18	76
4:5–6	122

❦

NEW TESTAMENT

Matthew
2:2	66
2:16–18	72
5:37	118
5:45	61
6	3
6:5–33	21
6:24	2, 20
6:25–27	2, 3
6:25–26	3
6:33	2, 4
7:7–11	9, 69
13:52	78
15	40
15:1–20	40
16:24–28	3
16:26	4
23	40
23:13–36	40
23:23–24	39
23:23	41
25:1–13	143
25:35–36	6
25:40	6
26:11	16

Mark
1:17–18	26
4:35–41	64
6:30–44	12
7:1–23	40
8:1–10	12
8:34—9:1	3
12:31	99
14:7	16

Luke
1:17	122
2:1–5	72
2:8	81
2:14–16	81
2:14	66
2:19–22	81
7:22	66
9:18–20	122
9:23–27	3
9:30	122
10:17–19	75
10:20	75
12:13–21	59, 60
12:15	59
12:22–31	60
12:22–25	2
12:24	60
15:4	137
16:1–9	21
16:13	2, 20
23:5–6	81

John
10:11–18	77
10:7–18	108

Acts
1:6	84

Scripture Index

Acts (*continued*)
4:32–35	92
4:32	94
4:33	94, 96
4:34	94
5	95
5:1–11	95
10	34
10:25	34

Romans
	101
1:26–27	102
4:17	103

1 Corinthians
4:7	67
13:13	40

Galatians
	101
3:28	100, 101

Ephesians
3:20–21	8–9
4:23–24	121

Revelation
3:5	76
13:8	76

www.ingramcontent.com/pod-product-compliance
Lightning Source LLC
Chambersburg PA
CBHW020830190426
43197CB00037B/1095